How to Say More While Speaking Less

A Guide to
Creating Effective Presentations

By Rick Flowers

Cover art drawn by Ryan Martin

Printed by
Maverick Publications
P.O. Box 5007
Bend, Oregon 97708

To my mother Anne, who taught me how to communicate, my wife Holly, who taught me the importance of good communication, and my children Jeff and Kristen who taught me that communication is a skill that you should never stop trying to improve.

PREFACE

In the 30+ years that I have been involved in public speaking, I have come to one inescapable conclusion. Most presenters do far more talking than they have to. This book is dedicated to the principle that *you can say more while speaking less.*

A presentation should be designed to deliver a message, and an effective presentation is one in which that message is delivered effectively. All to often in public speaking the message that a presenter wishes to convey gets lost somewhere in the process. Maybe the message is surrounded by so much unessential data that it loses its effectiveness, or maybe the speaker himself sabotages his own message by not delivering it in the most exciting manner. Regardless of the reasons, a presentation that fails to hit the target, wastes the time of the speaker, and more importantly, wastes the time of the audience.

In this book I have addressed all the key areas that help determine a presentations effectiveness. These key areas are summed up in what I call the W.A.T.E.R. process, which consists of a **W**ell written presentation, **A**udience analysis, **T**aking control of your fear, **E**ffective speaking skills, and **R**ehearsal. While other books may also touch on these areas, the approach that this book takes is considerably different. In this book I look at presenting from the point of view of the audience.

Everything that a presenter does should be evaluated by how it affects the people listening. The purpose of a presentation is not just to look good! The purpose of a presentation in not just to sound good! The purpose of a presentation is to convey a message to one or more people.

This book discusses what is really important to a presentation. Specifically, it teaches that:

- You must start with a message that is simple and meaningful to the listener
- You must deliver this message in a clear and straightforward manner, and
- You must mix nonverbal elements into the presentation that are designed to either maintain the listeners interest or help define the message for the listener

By the end of this book you will find that you will be able to accomplish the purpose of your presentation in considerably less time than before, and with the added bonus that your message will be understood better and remembered longer by the audience.   By the end of this book you will truly know . . .

"HOW TO SAY MORE, WHILE SPEAKING LESS".

CONTENTS (PART I)

CHAPTER 1   INTRODUCTION

CHAPTER 2   TAKE CONTROL OF YOUR FEAR

CHAPTER 3   EFFECTIVE SPEAKING SKILLS

CHAPTER 4   EIGHT DOs AND DON'Ts

CONTENTS

CHAPTER 5   PROVIDING EFFECTIVE CONTENT

CHAPTER 6   PLANNING THE PRESENTATION

CHAPTER 7   PREPARING THE PRESENTATION

(PART II)

CHAPTER 8   PERSONALIZING THE PRESENTATION

CHAPTER 9   PRACTICING THE PRESENTATION

APPENDIX A   GOLDEN POINT REVIEW

APPENDIX B   REVIEW OF CONTENT LISTS

CHAPTER 1

INTRODUCTION

Picture this:

> *You arrive on time to a much-anticipated seminar, one that you have been looking forward to for quite some time. The presenter approaches the podium 10 minutes late, "stuck in traffic," he says. "Now, if I can just find my notes, we can get started." As the presenter proceeds with his program, you acknowledge to yourself that, yes, this is indeed the information you were looking for, but something is wrong. What is it? You just can't seem to get excited about the subject matter. The truth is -- you're bored to death!*
>
> *What was expected to be a stimulating and exciting approach to the subject has instead developed into a litany of dull data for you to digest. Your mind begins to wander and you find yourself glancing occasionally at your watch. The words, "So, in conclusion, I would like to say . . ." bring you back to reality, and you join the rest of the audience in polite applause as the presenter leaves the stage.*

We have all suffered through experiences like this. A presentation that misses the target happens far more often than any of us in the speaking profession care to admit. But why? What is it that makes some presentations come alive for the audience, while others just seem to be "dead on arrival." Throughout my over 30 years in public speaking, first as a classroom instructor, then as a member of the sales profession, I have spent considerable time both presenting to, and being part of, an audience. As a presenter I have had audiences give me standing ovations, as well as those whose reactions could best be described as "luke warm". In either case I took something from the situation that made me a better speaker. As a member of an audience, I have seen and heard many outstanding presenters and, unfortunately, far too many not-so-outstanding speakers. Again, I took something positive from each presentation. This book is based on a collection of those thoughts and experiences that I have used to influence my own presentation style.

PRESENTATION SKILLS: THE KEY TO SUCCESS

We all have the ability to communicate, and maybe it's because of this, that good communication skills are largely taken for granted. In an effort to rise to the top of their profession, people may dedicate themselves to years of education and on-the-job-training to acquire and refine the skills of their profession, and that's as it should be. Yet those same people will rarely spend any time working on the skills necessary to communicate effectively. . . and that's a big mistake.

Research by the American Society for Training and Development concluded that "*Specific job knowledge is the only thing that ranks above communication skills in determining workplace success.*" So it stands to reason that given a group of people who have equal job knowledge, those with the superior communication skills will have the far greater chance of succeeding.

Success is really what this book is all about! If you want to achieve success in your career, then you need the benefits that can be attained through good presentation skills. Benefits that will have people seeing you in a different light. It may happen slowly at first, but before long friends and coworkers will begin to see you as:

- *Being more credible* - Ask a group of good trial lawyers and they will be the first to admit that when two lawyers are arguing a point, and are inundating the jury with logic and facts, it is essentially the lawyer who comes across the best, the one that has the best presentation skills, that most often gets credited with having the most credible arguments, and being the most believable.

- *Being more persuasive* - Successful salesmen know that in selling, it is often more important how you present your product, and how you present yourself, than what specific features your product may actually possess. Have you ever heard the expression: "This product is so good it sells itself"? Not true, in sales it is mostly the better communicator not the better product that wins out in the end.

- *Being more competent* - Politicians are particularly sensitive to the fact that If you appear poised and self-assured while speaking in public, people will tend to judge you more favorably on all aspects of your competency. In fact, for politicians, speaking skills determine 99% of their effectiveness. (This is often called people skills, but it is, in reality, presentation skills whether you're speaking one on one, or to a group).

- *Having more leadership skills* - Top corporate executives know that, in many business situations, the difference between success and failure rests with their ability to communicate effectively to those around them. To put it another way, effective presentation skills can (and does) create a direct path to corporate power.

Good lawyers do it, successful salesmen do it, politicians do it, and top corporate executives do it. Virtually every successful person utilizes effective speaking. It too can be the key that unlocks the doors to your success. Speaking well is synonymous with winning and we can all be winners!

EFFECTIVE PRESENTATIONS

What is an effective presentation? This is not an easy question to answer. Throughout this book I will be spending a substantial amount of time discussing the key points that influence a presentation's effectiveness. You will find that much of this book examines these points from the point of view of the speaker. This is only natural since the goal of this book is to make you, the reader, a more effective presenter. The problem with this "speaker centric" focus, however, is that it does not take into consideration either the attitudes of the listener, or the complexity of the message that the speaker is trying to be convey. I like to think of an effective presentation as more like a 3-ring circus with the message in the center ring.

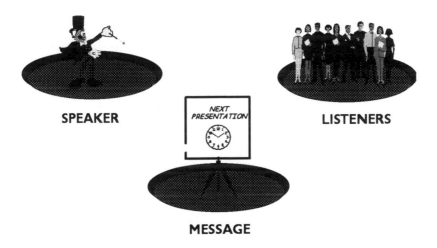

Figure 1A

Even though both the listener and the speaker share a common message they may end up with quite different opinions on what it takes to make that message effective. The listener's viewpoint is more likely to involve the "form" of the presentation rather than the substance. While a speaker's view may be just the opposite, with the focus typically being centered on the information presented.

The truth is, that while they are both right,, the presenter and the listener are concentrating on totally different components of the communication process. An effective presentation cannot be accomplished by looking exclusively at the perspective of the audience, or the perspective of the speaker. We must instead blend the perspectives of each.

The Audience Perspective

Inherently we all have some idea of what it takes to make a presentation effective, even if we have never presented to a group before. There are several reasons for this. The most important of which is that we have all had substantial experience being part of an audience. The ample time which we have spent in classrooms, attending seminars, or watching political speeches and debates on television, has given each and every one of us a unique perspective of what an effective presentation should be.

If this perspective alone provided us the with all the information we needed to make our own presentations effective, then there would be little need for this book. We could simply "tap" into this knowledge and adjust our behavior accordingly. Unfortunately, there is much more to an effective presentation than what we see as a member of the audience. The problem with looking at an effective presentation from the point of view of the listener then, is that much of the important information is missing.

It sort of reminds me of the Supreme Court decision in the early 1960's regarding pornography. Remember? The Supreme Court said in effect, *"We can't define pornography, but we know it when we see it."* I believe that the reactions of an audience attending a presentation are very much like those of the Supreme Court, *they can't define an effective presentation, they just know one when they see it.* This is because, from a listener's point of view, many of those things that actually make a presentation effective go unnoticed. You rarely find a listener thinking, "Gee, I really got sucked in by that opening," or "Gosh, this presentation is really well organized." Listeners don't think, "That was a dynamic closing." They just think, "That was a dynamic speaker."

On the other hand, a listener has no problem knowing what makes a presentation bad. Bad presentations, and a bad presenter, are instantly recognizable. If the listener is concentrating on the speaker's technique, or lack of it, instead of focusing on the message that is being delivered, then that speaker has already lost half the battle.

The Speaker's Perspective

Throughout my career, I have seen many speakers who, when they finished their presentations, felt very good about their effectiveness. Some speakers felt they were effective because the just didn't "mess up". While other speakers felt that they were effective because they were able to include as much information into their presentations as time would allow. Some speakers felt that they were effective if the audience didn't seem to have any questions when they finished. Still other speakers felt they were effective if there were many questions when they finished.

Were any of these presentations truly effective? *Well maybe*, but what if the audience did not come away from the presentation with the message that the speaker was trying to convey. What if they got bored, and started daydreaming? What if the audience failed to comprehend the key points of the presentation? What if the audience got overloaded and "tuned out" much of the information? Would the presentations have been effective then? *Of course not.*

The problem with looking at a presentation's effectiveness from the speaker's perspective is that it does not take into consideration the needs of the audience.

The Combined Perspective

It is important to know that the purpose of a presentation is not just to *look good*. The purpose of a presentation is not just to *sound good*. The purpose of a presentation is to convey a message, and an effective presentation conveys that message effectively. This can only be done when the perspective of the speaker is in balance with the perspective of the audience.

Some speakers feel that the "words" of their presentation are all that they need to be successful. They are wrong! In an effective presentation, speakers accomplish their goals by providing their message in a form that the listeners can understand and relate to. To accomplish this, it is necessary that speakers spend just as much time thinking about how the message will be received, as they do in formulating what "words" the message will consist of.

Throughout this book we will be discussing "GOLDEN POINTS". Points which provide helpful hints concerning all aspects of an effective presentation. This would be an appropriate time for our first GOLDEN POINT:

GOLDEN POINT #1:

AN EFFECTIVE PRESENTATION IS ONE IN WHICH THE LISTENER BOTH RECEIVES AND UNDERSTANDS THE SPEAKER'S MESSAGE

Figure 1B

This means that, just as beauty is in the eyes of the beholder, a good or bad presentation is determined by the listener. As Marjorie Brody wrote in her book PowerPresentations, "*...effective speaking is an audience centered sport.*" I couldn't agree more! It is up to us, the presenters to understand that a presentation is no better or no worse than how it is perceived by the audience. They are real people, and they are the sole judges of your performance.

HOW DO YOU ACHIEVE EFFECTIVE PRESENTATION SKILLS?

The answer is much easier than you might imagine. The first step is to do what you have already decided to do - - *get the information*. It is not important whether this information comes to you through seminars, books like this one, or just the school of "hard knocks", the important thing is to get it. Information is the seed we must plant before we can realistically develop any skill or expertise we desire. And just as a seed needs water to grow and flourish, water, as it so happens, is the key ingredient in the development of superior presentation skills. I'm not talking about water...
...I'm talking about *W.A.T.E.R.*. the five steps to achieving a successful presentation:

WELL WRITTEN PRESENTATION

AUDIENCE ANALYSIS

TAKE CONTROL OF YOUR FEAR

EFFECTIVE SPEAKING SKILLS

REHEARSE, REHEARSE, REHEARSE

Figure 1C

W.A.T.E.R. represents the keys to effective speaking. And just like real water, our *W.A.T.E.R.*. can be a friend, and make even the most difficult presentation a "piece of cake"...

W.A.T.E.R CAN BE A FRIEND. . .

Figure 1D

. . .or it can be an enemy.   A constant reminder of why a particular presentation falls "flat" and fails to accomplish its purpose.

. . . OR AN ENEMY

Figure 1E

You see, what W.A.T.E.R. really makes us do, is concentrate on the most important aspects of presentations. Taking into consideration all factors than influence the effectiveness of our presentations. To understand these factors, it is necessary to take a closer look at what communication really is.

THE COMMUNICATION PROCESS

Communication is composed of three interrelated elements: The Verbal, the Vocal, and the Visual.

The message contained in any presentation is the sum total of what you say (verbal), how you say it (vocal), and what image you project as you're saying it (visual). All are important to an effective presentation, *but which is the most important?* A study by the University of California Los Angeles, specifically designed to determine which of these factors had the most influence on a group of listeners, had a surprising result. It indicated that the verbal portion of the message accounted for only 7% of the total impact on the audience, with the non-verbal portion of the message (visual and vocal) accounted for the other 93%! While there is no doubt that both the content and delivery are essential to a presentation, clearly the delivery is the key to making that presentation effective.

Figure 1F

One of the most dramatic events that tends to support the results of this study happened in 1960 presidential campaign. In the midst of a very close race, John F. Kennedy and Richard M. Nixon agreed to a series of three televised debates. With much of the country either watching on TV or listening on the radio, the first debate was held. Nothing seemed out of the ordinary, until well after the debate when the media started conducting their polls to find out who the winner was. Then something completely unexpected happened. It seemed, most of the people who listened to that first debate on the radio thought that Nixon was a clear winner, while those who watched the debate on television thought that Kennedy had won. Why? What was different in the perceptions of the two audiences? Obviously it was the *visual* portion that made the difference. Somehow the words spoken by a young, handsome John Kennedy had more impact on the viewers than it did on the listeners. In fact, what the viewers saw was a stark difference between the two candidates. Kennedy looked confident and poised, his dark suit contrasting against a gray background. Richard Nixon on the other hand looked ill-at-ease, beads of perspiration forming on his upper lip, while his light gray suit seemed to blend into the background. These debates changed, not only the face of politics, but the face of public speaking forever.

Non-Verbal Communication

A presentation is composed of a group of words, but the message contained in that presentation is derived from much more than just the words that are spoken (93% vs. 7%). Words themselves do not have meaning. It is, in reality, the listener who assigns the meaning to each and every word spoken. Sometimes that meaning coincides with the speaker's intent, and sometimes it doesn't. Therefore, the use of words alone cannot guarantee that our message will be understood, we need more.

In order to accurately convey a message, the speaker must be able to supplement the words he uses. This is done through non-verbal communication. Non-verbal communication allows the presenter to influence the listener's perceptions of the verbal message contained in the presentation. A good presenter has the ability to go beyond the "words" of his presentation, and instead, conveys meaning by the way he uses those words, the tone of his voice, and the body language he exhibits. Having been married for nearly 25 years, I can certainly endorse the importance of non-verbal communication. When the question of, *"What's the matter?"* is met with the answer, *"nothing"*, you can be assured that verbal communication means very little. It is the non-verbal clues which provides the true response.

A strong non-verbal presence can be used to convey confidence, authority and expertise. A slightly milder presence can be used to create a calming effect and provide an environment that fosters teamwork and interaction. A more detailed discussion on non-verbal communications is given in chapter 3.

Verbal Communication

When it comes to public speaking, there is an old saying, *"Good speaking skills will never save a bad presentation."* Although verbal communication accounts for only 7% of the total effectiveness of a presentation, its significance cannot be ignored. An effective presentation must begin with a strong verbal message before a presenter can have any hope of using his non-verbal skills to create an impact. The verbal message delivered by a presenter must be simple, direct, and to-the-point. All the non-verbal techniques in the world will have little effect, if the listener does not comprehend the basic points brought out in the presentation.

W.A.T.E.R. AND THE COMMUNICATION PROCESS

The five keys to a successful presentation discussed earlier, are designed to aid in the communication process. A *Well Written Presentation*, combined with an appropriate amount of *Audience Analysis*, produces the content necessary to make the verbal portion of your presentation truly outstanding. *Taking Control of Your Fear* and utilizing *Effective Speaking Techniques* will allow you to maximize your delivery and make the most of the non-verbal aspects of communications. Finally, when *Rehearsal* is added to the process you will have a formula for achieving an effective presentation.

In the two parts of this book each of these keys to an effective presentation will be discussed in greater detail. In PART I, we will begin with the factors that have the most influence on the non-verbal part of the communication process. Namely, how to <u>Take Control of Your Fear,</u> and <u>Effective Speaking Skills.</u> PART II of this book then continues with those factors that influence the Verbal part of the communication process, <u>Developing the Presentation,</u> and <u>Analyzing the Audience</u>.

PART 1

THE
DELIVERY

CHAPTER 2

TAKE CONTROL

OF YOUR FEAR

So, you say you get a little nervous when you speak in front of a group. You get those butterflies in your stomach, you begin to perspire just a little, and your face turns a distinct shade of red. Well, welcome to the club! Fear is a normal reaction to the pressures of public speaking. Anyone who claims not to be nervous prior to a presentation is either lying to themselves, or lying to us. In fact, a recent ABC News program estimated that over 12 million people suffer from severe stage fright!

Winston Churchhill, who is recognized by many as one of the 20th century's finest speakers, consistently had to fight the battle of nerves each and every time he spoke in public. In fact his fear was so pervasive, that as a young member of the House Of Commons, he actually fainted from acute anxiety while attempting to deliver a speech.

The fear generated by just the thought of presenting to a group is so common, that not only did it make the list of the 14 worst human fears, *it was ranked #1*. Fear of public speaking, in fact, was ranked well ahead of Death which was only #6 on the list.

WORST HUMAN FEARS

1.	**PUBLIC SPEAKING**	**41%**
2.	HEIGHTS	32%
3.	INSECTS AND BUGS	22%
3.	FINANCIAL PROBLEMS	22%
3.	DEEP WATER	22%
6.	SICKNESS	19%
6.	DEATH	19%
8.	FLYING	18%
9.	LONELINESS	14%
10.	DOGS	11%
11.	DRIVING/RIDING IN A CAR	9%
12.	DARKNESS	8%
12.	ELEVATORS	8%
14.	ESCALATORS	5%

Figure 2A

Fear is our body's normal response to a potential threat. Each individual may notice that this fear can take on several different forms and intensities depending upon their background and experience. It also tends to come in many disguises. An actor may refer to it as *"stage fright"*. A bride on her wedding day may experience feelings of *"anxiety"*, while her groom may feel a particular *"restlessness"*, an athlete may just notice that he gets especially *"psyched"* up before the big game, and to a presenter, well to a presenter, it is just plain old *"nervousness"*. They are all the same fear response and it will never completely go away. Nor do we want it to. Having fear shows that you are concerned and that you want to do a good job. Having fear means that you care about the outcome of your speech and that you want to do your very best.

Now here is something that may surprise you. The feeling of fear is actually beneficial to your performance. Once you learn to control the fear your presentation will be better because of it. It is important to understand that the body, in response to the fear, produces adrenaline, helping you get the "edge" that you need to be at your best. The end result is that your mind reacts quicker, your enthusiasm will be greater, and your conviction stronger.

The goal of a presenter then, is not to eliminate the fear but to control it. Which happens to be GOLDEN POINT #2.

Figure 2B

The main question then, is how do you control that fear? An important part of learning to control your fear is to understand what causes the fear in the first place. To begin with, let's look at fear as an acronym **F.E.A.R.,** standing for False Expectations Appearing Real. In most cases, it is not the act of public speaking that causes fear, after all we speak to people all day long and think nothing of it. It is the *expectation* of possible undesirable results that creates our anxiety, or to put it another way, we are afraid of what *might happen*.

Let's say we are afraid of looking foolish, or possibly "drawing a blank" while speaking. The mere thought of this creates an *expectation* in our minds. Our subconscious minds can dwell on those expectations to such an extent that we start to believe that they are indeed real. This causes us to experience the physiological reactions of those undesirable results before we even get up to speak. It is at this point that our conscience mind must step in and recognize whether or not the reactions we are experiencing have any validity.

Fear begins to become a problem when those reactions are allowed to go unchecked to the point that it actually results in aiding the very expectations that we were worried about in the first place. This has a tendency to enhance the original fear and continues the cycle until the fear is abated. This is referred to as the "Fear Triangle, and is illustrated in figure 2C.

Figure 2C

When Roosevelt said *"We have nothing to fear, but fear itself"*. He could easily have been talking about public speaking. You see, it is sometimes the fear of undesirable results that creates the environment that can actually cause the undesirable results.

WHAT ARE YOU AFRAID OF?

Politicians earn their livelihood by speaking in public. Of the millions of speeches given by tens of thousands of politicians throughout history, two particular speeches come to mind. The first was the inaugural address by William Henry Harrision, the second was a speech given by Senator, and former Vice President Alben W. Barkley.

These two speeches come to mind not because of their particular eloquence, or their unique call to action, but because in each case the speech itself may have contributed to the death of the speaker. When William Henry Harrison gave his inaugural address in cold, rainy, January weather without wearing a hat, he was viewed as a rugged *"man of the people*". When he died of pneumonia less than a month later, many people considered the almost 3 hour speech to be his undoing.

With Senator Alben W. Barkley, it was even more dramatic. As a career Politician, and former vice-president of the United States, Barkley had given thousands of speeches on almost any subject imaginable. While giving a speech at Washington and Lee University he suffered a fatal heart attack. Whether it was the speech itself, or a combination of his advanced age (he was 79) and the fact that he had recently married a woman 33 years his junior, is not important. What is important is that he *died while making a speech.*

I like to tell these stories only to illustrate a particular point. As long as you remember to wear a hat, and as long as you're married to someone your own age, then the chances are pretty good that you are going to survive the ordeal.

So what is it about public speaking that you're really afraid of? If you're like most speakers, your fear tends to revolve around four areas:

(1) Fear of Making a Mistake / Looking foolish

Let's face it, to a certain degree, this fear accompanies almost any task we undertake. No one wants to look foolish. In public speaking, however, this fear tends to take on even larger proportions. One of the reasons for this is that most novice presenters feel that their objective is to make the *"perfect"* speech, and that means that they can never make a mistake. I'm here to tell you that *it's okay if you make a mistake.* Giving a speech is a human activity and making mistakes comes with the territory. If you are well prepared, you have your facts straight, and the presentation itself is well organized, then any mistakes you make along the way will not make you look foolish. In fact, most mistakes made during a presentation either go unnoticed, or have very little impact on the audience. It is our own ego that overreacts to the slightest mistake. One of the reasons that I utilize videotape so much in my workshops is to illustrate to presenters just how unnoticeable some mistakes actually are. After presenting, a speaker can usually list the places where he stumbled over a particular word, lost his place, or had unanticipated pauses to collect his thoughts.

Each of these *mistakes* tends to get magnified in the mind of the speaker. When the recorded speech is played back, the speaker is usually the most surprised person in the room. Those pauses that seemed to last forever are, for the most part, non-existent, and the places where a speaker lost his place and deviated from the script, flowed as smoothly as if it were originally written that way.

(2) Fear of Being Judged by the Audience

When some presenters stand up in front of an audience they have a tendency to believe that the whole world is not only looking at them, but judging them as well. Soon they begin to feel that they are alone, at center-stage, with a giant spotlight shinning on them. In many ways they are right. A good presenter should have a "stage presence" and command the attention of the audience, but a good presenter also knows that even though the spotlight is on him, he is not necessarily alone. Remember, a presentation is a collaborative effort between the audience and the presenter.

The truth is, the audience is not keying in on every word the presenter says, looking for mistakes or contradictions. The audience genuinely wants the speaker to succeed. First of all, consider the fact that the audience is at your presentation for a reason, more than likely to learn the information that you are there to present. Secondly, a high degree of empathy exists between the audience and the speaker. People in the audience have a tendency to picture themselves in the speaker's place. When the speaker is going well the audience enjoys the presentation, but when the speaker begins to fumble, or forgets what he has to say and panics, the audience will begin to feel just as uncomfortable as the speaker.

So It's important for you, the presenter, to understand that the spotlight really is, where it should be, equally divided between you, the audience, and the subject matter that you and the audience have in common. Before you know it, both you and the audience will be so in tuned to the subject that you'll actually enjoy the spotlight.

(3) Fear That Our Points Will Be Rejected

What if the audience doesn't agree with the main points of our presentation? This can cause worry to even the most experienced presenter. This fear is especially significant in a business setting where the audience may be composed largely of your peers and supervisors. Since not every presentation can be guaranteed to hit the mark with 100% of the audience, 100% of the time, what is really at the root of our fear?

I believe that what we are really afraid of is that if our points are rejected as being invalid or unimportant, then it reflects on us. It means that we as people, are invalid, or unimportant. Nothing can be further from the truth. A good presentation has just the opposite effect. When a presentation is done well, it adds credibility to the presenter and this credibility is, for the most part, independent of whether or not the audience agrees with facts that the presenter offers. Comments like, *"you've obviously researched your points well"*, or *" Gee, I never thought of it that way before"*, means that you have been effective in your presentation.

(4) Fear of Boring the Audience

This of course, goes back to the feeling that we are at "center stage". As long as we feel that the spotlight is on us, we want to be successful. We as presenters want the audience hanging on every word. The truth of the matter, however, is that commanding complete attention for long periods of time is extremely difficult. Most of this book, in fact, is geared to providing hints and techniques that will allow us to do just that.

CONTROLLING THE FEAR

Unfortunately, understanding what causes the fear does not eliminate it. It does, however, place that fear in the proper perspective thus giving us the opportunity to control it. One first important step in the control of fear is to understand that it does not remain constant. The intensity or our fear, and therefore the amount of control needed, will vary throughout the presentation. The first step in learning to control the fear, is to understand how the fear changes as we progress through the presentation.

As the chart illustrated in figure 2D indicates, fear begins before we even start the presentation. It continues to increase as the time for the presentation approaches and reaches its maximum as we first begin to speak. The good news is that the effect of fear almost always reduces to a very low level once we comfortably settle into the presentation.

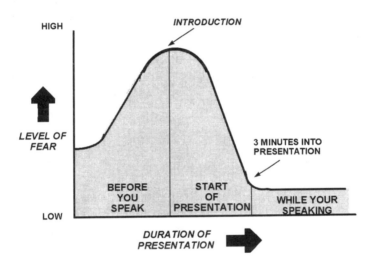

Figure 2D

In order to accurately discuss the idea of control, the chart further divides the "fear cycle" into 3 critical time periods. Time periods where the anxiety of the presenter will likely take on different forms, and require different control techniques. These three critical periods are:

- Before You Speak
- The Start of the Presentation
- While You're Speaking

Before You Speak

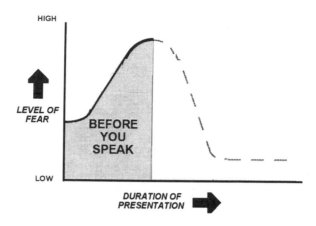

Figure 2E

The first critical period is illustrated in figure 2E. It represents that time prior to speaking, while you are either waiting for your introduction or waiting for the presentation to start. During this period it is likely that your fear will begin to rise. The closer you get to that start of your presentation, the more intense the fear may become. Don't be surprised if all of a sudden you find yourself hoping for a power outage, a fire alarm, or an earthquake. All good presenters will experience some apprehension immediately before speaking, it's only natural. Don't expect to eliminate this fear, accept it. Those "pre-presentation jitters" are a fact of life. There are however, several things you can do to keep this fear at a minimum.

- **Prepare** - There is nothing that reduces fear more than being prepared. Also, there is nothing that can add to your fear more than knowing that you're not as prepared as you could be. Once you've written and organized your presentation -- *practice*. Practice is the key to making a presentation effective. At least 3 to 5 practice rounds should precede every presentation. Whenever possible, you should attempt to arrive a least an hour before the presentation is to begin. This will not only give you time to insure that the room is set-up the way you want it, but it will also give you the time to perform at least one more practice session. This time, in the same room that your presentation will eventually be given.

- **Visualize success** - As John-Roger and Peter McWilliams so aptly put it in the title of their book, *you can't afford the luxury of a negative thought*. When it comes to speaking in public it is especially important to focus on the positive. While you're waiting for your presentation to begin, and those nagging doubts begin to creep into your mind, do what top athletes like gymnast Mary Lou Retton and golfer Tiger Woods do to enhance their performance. Use your "mind's eye" to visualize a successful presentation. See yourself delivering a top-notch presentation, being in control, and see the audience hanging on your every word. You may just find that your fear might be replaced with an eager anticipation to begin speaking.

- **Isometric Exercises** - Exercise is an excellent way of burning that nervous energy immediately before you begin to speak. It reduces the adrenaline that is most likely surging through your body, at this time. Of course, you can't get up and start doing jumping jacks before you speak, but you can create some of the same effects right there in your seat by using isometric exercises. Try taking your hands and pressing your palms together. Do this in short spurts lasting 4-5 seconds each and watch your nervousness begin to fade. Another great idea is to use your hands to grasp the bottom of your chair, then "lift up". Repeat this several times to relieve tension.

- **Deep Breathing** - When you get nervous, the first thing to suffer is your breathing. You tend not to take in as much oxygen as normal. Oxygen has a beneficial effect on your nervous system, and can help to relax you as you're waiting to begin your presentation. Breath deeply while still sitting in your chair, and especially just before you get up to speak. This will give a rush of oxygen into your blood stream. As you begin your presentation, continue this technique by pausing often and taking deep breaths each time.

When You Begin

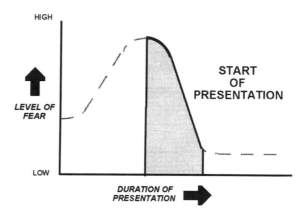

Figure 2F

Roscoe Drummond once wrote, *"the mind is a wonderful thing - it begins working the minute you're born, and doesn't stop until you get up to speak in public"*. As this quote so aptly describes, the second critical period that you need to get past is the start of the presentation, immediately following your introduction. It actually begins as you approach "center stage" and lasts for approximately 3 minutes. This is the most crucial period of the whole presentation. First of all, it corresponds to that point where your anxiety is most likely at its peak. It is also the period where the audience is forming its first impressions of both you and your presentation. The following hints will allow you safe passage through this period. Then, it won't be long before you notice that your "nerves" will start to settle down.

- **Act Confident** - A speaker, who approaches the presentation with confidence, rarely has to worry about fear. Resist any temptation to "share" with your audience the fact that you're nervous. It serves no useful purpose, and can only cause the listener to overreact to any minor mistakes you may end up making. The truth is that a nervous presenter will in fact make the audience nervous. No matter how nervous you may be, it is imperative that you "act" confident without crossing the line into arrogance. Remember, the mere fact that you're the one speaking indicates that you probably know more about the subject matter than anyone else in the room. The more confident the audience perceives you to be, the better your presentation will be received, and the quicker you will reach your own comfort zone.

- **Get Past the First 3 Minutes** - Whatever it takes, get past these first 3 minutes. I personally spend as much time practicing the first 3 minutes of my presentation as I do the rest of it. It may be a good idea in some cases to memorize your opening so that you can put yourself in "auto pilot" while you're waiting for your nerves to calm down. Another idea on getting past the first 3 minutes is to tell a joke or story that relates to the subject of the presentation.

- **Establish Eye Contact** - One sure way to calm your nerves, while making a positive impact on the audience is to establish eye contact from the moment you're introduced. As you walk to the podium or approach the front of the room, look at the listeners and try to establish that "visual bond" discussed earlier in this chapter.

- **Find the "Friendly Face"** - While you're establishing eye contact, look for a friendly face in the crowd. This may be someone you know, someone you may have met and talked with before the presentation, or just a member of the audience who seems to be giving you some extra positive feedback. As you begin your presentation, look at this individual several times to help calm those butterflies. This is a technique used by even the most experienced of speakers. In fact, take a tip from the President. Try to visualize the last time you watched the President of the United States give a major speech to congress. When he first approaches the podium the audience breaks out in applause, this applause is likely to last at least 3 minutes (no accident). While the applause is going on, what does the President do? Through his smile and finger pointing, he recognizes specific individuals in the audience -- the friendly faces. As he recognizes each friendly face his own anxiety begins to diminish.

While You're Speaking

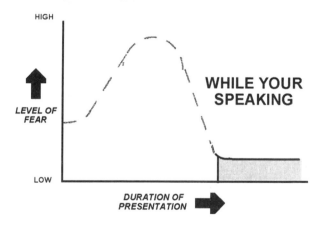

Figure 2G

As you're proceeding through those first 3 minutes, your fear will begin to fade. By the end of this period, you should be emotionally into the presentation with those butterflies all flying in formation. I like to call this period -- the comfort zone.

During this period of time, while you are delivering your presentation, there shouldn't be any room left for fear. Your mind instead is occupied, concentrating on the message that you are sending to the listeners. There are several things that you can do, however, to insure that your anxiety level remains low throughout the remainder of the presentation.

- **Be yourself** - Sounds easy, but many presenters approach a presentation as if they were reading a script written by someone else. Anytime you attempt to deliver a presentation that uses words, phrases, gestures or movements that are not normally a part of your personality, you run the risk of elevating your fear level. Stay within yourself and use your own experiences and background to make your points. You will feel more comfortable, and your presentation will be more believable because of it. Remember earlier in the chapter, the story about Winston Churchill fainting from anxiety? This was in his second speech to the House of Commons. In that speech he was attacking the financial policies of the current administration. A subject in which he was somewhat still a novice. The next time Winston Churchill got up to speak, he talked about himself and his war experiences from WWI. His anxiety level dropped to almost nothing, and he showed a confidence level that was lacking in the previous speech.

- **Move** - Staying "rigid" in one spot, such as behind a podium, can actually add to your fear. Body movement and hand gestures while you are delivering your presentation, on the other hand, can help to keep your level of fear to a minimum. As a presenter, you should move often to help relieve that nervous energy which was built up during the start of your presentation, but be careful to not "pace" or "rock", you still must move purposefully. I've seen many presenters who look as if they're either in a track meet, or in the waiting room at a hospital's maternity ward. This may help to calm the nerves of the presenter, but it drives the audience *NUTS*!

The chart below summarizes what we can do on both an emotional level and physical level to control the fear.

HOW TO CONTROL YOUR FEAR

	MENTALLY	*PHYSICALLY*
BEFORE YOU SPEAK	• Be Prepared • Visualize Success	• Isometric Exercise • Deep Breathing
AFTER YOUR INTRODUCTION	• Act Confident • Get Past the First 3 Minutes	• Establish Eye Contact • Look For the Friendly Face
WHILE YOU'RE SPEAKING	• Be Yourself	• Move Frequently

Chapter 3

Effective

Speaking Skills

The result of the UCLA study discussed in Chapter 1 indicated beyond any doubt that "*how*" you say something is far more important to the listener than "*what*" you say. As this study verified, the verbal portion of the presentation contributes only a small amount (7%) to the audience's understanding. While the vocal and visual elements that are contained in the non-verbal portion of the presentation, provide a significantly higher impact (93%). I relate the relative importance of verbal and non-verbal elements to the movie industry. Certainly, in order to produce an *Academy Award* caliber film, it takes a considerable amount of talent from the Actors, an excellent script from the Screenwriter, and a Director who can put the whole thing together. When the movie is a hit, however, who is deemed most responsible for the film's excellence? *The Director of course.* The Director is given credit for taking the script (the verbal element) and turning it into a powerful movie by controlling what we see and hear on the screen. You see, it's the Director who is responsible for the *way* the actors say their lines (the vocal element) and *what we see* as those lines are being said (the visual element). Ask any Producer for the key to an effective film and he will point to the Director as the one having the most control on its success or failure.

It is much the same situation in the world of public speaking. You are, in fact, the writer, actor, and director of your own presentation. Let the "director" in you come alive. Given the relative importance of non-verbal communication, its potential impact cannot be ignored in the delivery of your presentation. Like a movie director who controls what the audience sees and hears on the screen, the presenter must make maximum use of the non-verbal elements available to enhance the message of the presentation.

Spend time not only mastering the non-verbal forms of communication, but also using them in such a way as to define and clarify your verbal message. Your presentation will be better because of it.

As is illustrated below in GOLDEN POINT #3, a truly effective presentation is one in which we have all three elements of communication; the vocal, the visual and the verbal are supporting the same message to the audience. When this is done well, the communication process is operating at its optimum level, providing the audience with the greatest comprehension of the presentation's message.

Figure 3A

VOCAL SIGNALS

The vocal signals you provide while speaking must go hand-in-hand with the verbal portion of your presentation in defining your message to the listener. Although these vocal signals are oral in nature, they are considered non-verbal because they go beyond the "words" to both heighten and clarify your message. An effective speaker is able to use the vocal portion of his presentation to bring the "words" to life, and to keep the audience interested. Some of these vocal techniques involve the following:

- Voice Qualities
- Articulation
- Pronunciation
- Pauses and Timing

VOCAL SIGNALS - MUCH TO THINK ABOUT

Figure 3B

Voice Qualities

Vocal qualities such as Pitch, Inflection, Volume, and Rate can be used to create variety in our voice. Variety which is essential, in the generation, and maintaining of interest in the verbal portion of our presentation. Additionally, the voice qualities you posses, when properly used, can go a long way in projecting your enthusiasm and excitement to the listener.

This is important because, no matter how committed you are to the subject matter, it your voice doesn't appear enthusiastic and excited it will be difficult to convey that commitment to the audience.

- **Pitch** - It is necessary to alter the pitch of your voice in order to maintain interest. A monotone speaker has little chance of getting his message across to the listener. Think of pitch as the "music" in your voice, and just as music varies it's notes to create a song, the speaker must vary his pitch in delivering the presentation.

  Changing pitch can make a phrase become considerably more exciting and memorable. Try reading the phrase in example #1a out loud:

EXAMPLE #1a:

President Clinton is a great communicator. He has the ability to lead his followers, and inspire them with just the right words.

  Now try reading the same statement again, this time using a slight inflection to emphasize the words that are underlined in example #1b.

EXAMPLE #1b:

President Clinton is a <u>great</u> communicator. He has the ability to <u>lead</u> his followers, and <u>inspire</u> them with just the right words.

  As with example #1b, presenters will often underline the words in their notes that require special emphasis

- **Inflection** - The changing of pitch in order to convey a specific message is referred to as inflection. Inflection gives an added sense of meaning to a word or phrase and helps the listener interpret your message.

Take the previous statement used in example #1a and #1b. On the face of it, this statement seems quite a complement to President Clinton. That is until example #1c, when a Republican might repeat the same phrase, this time using a slight inflection to emphasize the words that are underlined.

EXAMPLE #1c:

<u>President</u> Clinton is a great communicator. He has the ability to lead <u>his</u> followers, and inspire them with <u>just</u> the right words.

Is that Republican saying that President Clinton is doing something now that he never was able to do as Governor? Is the speaker also implying that Clinton could lead only his followers and no one else? Finally, does the speaker indicate that there are no actions behind President Clinton's words? It is all in the inflection used by the speaker.

Everything I ever needed to know about the use of inflection, I learned from my daughter. While listening to her on a recent phone call with one of her friends, she successfully held up her end of the conservation for several minutes by just saying the word *"Oh"*. Figure 3C shows just some of the many different messages that can be sent just by using "Oh".

- "To Bad!"
- "You're Joking, Right?"
- "I See What You Mean"
- "That's Interesting, Tell Me More"
- "That's A Good Idea"

Figure 3C

Each different meaning is established through the use of different inflections. What inflection would you use to generate the correct corresponding meaning?

- **Volume** - Volume is probably the single most important factor in making your presentation intelligible to the audience. People cannot understand what they can't hear. Therefore, a presenter must make a conscious effort to regulate his volume throughout the presentation. Begin by adjusting your voice volume to the size of the room and the needs of the audience. Then as you present, read the body language and facial expressions of the audience to see if you're being heard. It should never be necessary to ask if the listeners can hear you -- a good presenter will adjust as needed.

  Another consideration regarding volume is that listeners will often use the presenter's volume as a non-verbal clue to help in analyzing the message. A speaker who speaks loud enough to be heard projects confidence to the audience. A speaker who speaks softly or mumbles may project just the opposite, causing the listeners to question the speaker's commitment to the subject matter presented.

- **Rate** - The speed at which we deliver our words will also have a direct impact on the success of the presentation. A presenter, who speaks too fast, may have trouble being understood by the audience. While a speaker who speaks too slowly may find that the listeners will have trouble maintaining their concentration throughout the presentation. A usually accepted rate of speaking during a presentation is between 120 - 150 words per minute. The exact rate used in a presentation however, will vary depending on the speaker and the type subject matter being presented. A presentation that is given to entertain can afford to be given at a much higher rate that one that is given to inform. Especially if the later is comprised of highly technical information.

Remember, the rate at which you speak, just as any of the other vocal qualities we've discussed, is part of the message you're sending to the audience. It must not only support the verbal message, but also enhance it. Use the rate at which you speak to help deliver your message by altering it throughout the presentation. Variety and change of pace can keep the listeners on their toes and help in the audience's overall understanding of your speech.

Articulation

Articulation, or enunciation, refers to the crispness and precision that we use in the forming of our words. Most of us are "lip lazy" in our normal conversation, dropping syllables and slurring sounds. Through years of neglect many of us have formed bad speech habits such as:

Dropped Endings	**Go-in** instead of **Going**	I'm *go-in* to the department store.
Altered Sounds	**Git** instead of **get**	It's time to *git* educated
Combining Sounds	Ja instead of **did you**	*Ja* ever wonder what makes the sky blue?
Reversing Sounds	**Perscription** instead of **prescription**	The doctor wrote me a *perscription*
Dropping Sounds	**Pitcher** instead of **picture**	One *pitcher* is worth a thousand words

The good news is that articulation is the easiest of all the vocal qualities to perfect. It involves nothing more than paying attention to your speech and eliminating whichever bad habits you may have developed. Listen to yourself as you speak, or better yet record yourself, and look out for some of the types of articulation errors illustrated above. And for heaven sake, never ask "Could *ja git* me the camera, I'm *gonna* take a *pitcher*?"

Pronunciation

Related to the idea of articulation, is that of pronunciation. To be understood, not only must you be careful to form the sounds correctly, but it is essential that the audience understand which words you are trying to say. The key is in the audience's *understanding*. A presenter must be aware of how he pronounces certain words, and whether this pronunciation is understandable to the audience. This does not mean that an effective speaker must be free of any accents, speaking only with the traditional "Midwestern" flair. Regional and foreign accents are not necessarily a barrier to communication. In fact, two of the best speakers I've heard, Reverend Jesse Jackson and Zig Ziglar, use their accents quite effectively. For most of us, however, pronunciation is yet another non-verbal key that the audience uses to evaluate our message. Negative judgments based on our pronunciation of certain words can stand in the way of effective communication. If you're not sure how to pronounce a word, either don't use it or look it up. Avoid risking pronunciation errors, which the audience can interpret as a sign of ignorance or lack of preparation.

Pauses and Timing

Most novice presenters think that, since their purpose is to speak, it is incumbent on them to make sure that they "fill" any available time with the sound of their own voice. This couldn't be further from the truth. Sometimes, as the saying goes, *silence is golden*, and silence in the form of pauses can be a highly effective means of communication when used correctly. Pauses are to a speech, what punctuation marks are to the written word. Pauses can be used to add emphasis to the main points in your speech as well as letting the audience know that you have come to the end of a thought. The pause gives the audience time to reflect on what you have just said as well as indicating it's importance. One technique that I used quite frequently during my years as a technical instructor was to verbalize an important point and pause for a time to let that point sink in, after the pause I would say, "*let me repeat that*", and proceed to repeat the point again. I guarantee that every student in the room immediately recognized the importance placed on that point and took notes accordingly.

Pauses can also be quite effective in getting the listener's attention. When you think that many in the audience may be "drifting off" while you're speaking, a pause can actually bring them back to being an active listener. A listeners normal first reaction when you stop speaking will be to "replay" the last few sentences in their head and evaluate the point that you, as the speaker, were trying to make. Now that you have them back, you can continue with your presentation. Be careful here to insure that the pause makes sense in the scope of your presentation, otherwise those in the audience who were actively following your message may be confused by an inappropriate pause.

Nothing is more powerful than the "dramatic pause" during your delivery to generate interest in your subject matter. Pauses are particularly effective prior to the climax of a story or after asking the audience a question, even if that question is rhetorical in nature. In either case the presenter uses the pause to generate anticipation within the listener which then can be satisfied after the pause.

Some final words on maximizing the effectiveness of pauses. First the "don'ts". Don't use pauses too often, (too many pauses can make the presenter look artificially manipulative), don't let the pause last too long (a pause of 3 - 5 seconds should be adequate in most instances), and finally, don't lower your eyes during the pause (loss of eye contact with the audience can reduce any impact created by the pause itself). Now the "Do's". Do use the pause as a method of relaxing and collecting your thoughts for the next part of the presentation. You may even use the pause as a means to quickly glance at your notes, or, if you have ventured away from the podium, the pause can give you the added time necessary to return to your notes before you begin a new point.

VISUAL SIGNALS

We have all seen speakers who command attention the moment they open their mouths to speak, we sometimes refer to this as "presence" or "charisma". There just seems to be an instant chemistry that exists with the listener. In many ways this is an accurate analogy. Just as chemistry utilizes the combination of several different chemicals to achieve the desired result, presenters utilize a combination of visual signals to maximum their effectiveness and create that intangible feeling within the audience

The visual signals we provide during a presentation, according to Dr. Albert Mehrabian's UCLA study, account for over half (55%) of the total message we convey to the audience. More importantly, during those first 7 seconds, while the audience is creating its important first impressions of us, these visual signals can account for nearly 100% of our total impact. This makes visual signals the primary factor in the success or failure of our message reaching the audience. Many times an otherwise good presentation can be sabotaged by the visual signals we send as part of the message. If it is important that the vocal signals be in concert with the verbal message, then it is even more imperative that the visual signals also support that same message. Does the audience get the impression that we're excited about the subject matter that we're presenting? Do they see us as experienced, qualified presenters? Do they recognize us as experts in the subject matter being presented? The answer to all these questions can very well depend on the visual signals we provide during the presentation.

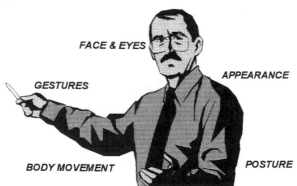

VISUAL SIGNALS - THE KEY TO UNDERSTANDING

Figure 3D

Visual signals are sent in many forms. Some of the key signals are sent through the following:

- Face & Eyes
- Gestures
- Posture
- Body Movement
- Appearance

Face & Eyes

The most important of all visual signals are done with the face and eyes. Through facial expressions you, as the presenter, can communicate a significant amount of information to the listener. First, your face reveals much about yourself and your feelings as they relate the presentation itself. A good presenter will use his facial expressions to let the audience know that he's happy to be there, that he's comfortable with the subject matter, and that he believes in what he's presenting. A smile is really the presenter's best friend in this situation, it should be used early and often throughout the presentation.

Secondly, facial expressions can be used to establish a sort of "visual bonding" with the audience. The presenter reads the reactions to his presentation from the faces of the listeners, while they in turn use the facial expressions of the presenter to help in interpreting the verbal message being provided. Be aware of your facial expressions and pay particular attention to them as you prepare and rehearse your presentation.

Of all the features of the face, none is more expressive than the eyes. It is also the key to "visual bonding" with the audience as described above. A presenter who looks at the floor or ceiling, or focuses on the wall in the back of the room is not relating to the audience. He is perceived as talking *at* them not *to* them. Without relating to the audience there cannot be true "visual bonding" and the communication of the verbal message will be affected. In order to achieve "visual bonding" the presenter must make an effort to establish eye contact with the audience. In small groups this is relatively easy, but in a larger group it can be quite tricky to establish eye contact with each and every listener. One way of doing this might be to pick out several people, located in different sections of the audience. Establish eye contact with the person in the first location for approximately 3 to 5 seconds and move on to the next location. It is important that as you move to the next location, you slowly scan across the audience as opposed to any quick movements. This gives each listener the illusion that you are talking directly to them. When you have completed your eye contact with the last section, start over and continue the same sequence throughout the presentation.

One more word about eye contact, be careful not to fall into the trap that I have seen with many novice presenters. During a presentation, a presenter will single out a member of the audience for a disproportionate amount of eye contact. This usually occurs when the presenter finds one member of the audience who provides considerably more positive feedback to the presenter than the other listeners. Affirmative feedback in the form of nodding or smiling can attract the presenter's attention like a magnet. Before, too long it will begin to look as if the presenter is doing a "one-on-one" with that listener.

Gestures

Another powerful tool in the arsenal of visual signals is the use of gestures. A gesture is a purposeful movement, which is designed to support or illustrate the ideas contained in the verbal message. In other words, gestures allow the presenter to associate some sort of action with the words that are being used. Gestures enhance the presentation on three different levels. First, it helps to clarify the verbal message by reinforcing the key points of the presentation and making them more meaningful to the audience. Second, gestures tend to add a certain amount of energy to the presentation, which will help maintain the audience's attention. Finally, gestures can help the presenter relax as it answers the age-old question of what to do with your hands.

There are several key rules concerning gestures that must be taken into consideration. The first is that, when it comes to gestures, the only thing worse than none is *too many*. Use gestures only to clarify key ideas, or emphasize certain points. Hands that are in constant motion will only distract from the presentation. Gestures should be designed to support the verbal message, not overwhelm it.

Another rule concerning the use of gestures is that they should be spontaneous, or at least appear that way. The use of "canned", rehearsed gestures may still clarify key ideas, but it will do nothing for the excitement and energy contained in the presentation. Nothing is more noticeable than a presenter who has prepared himself to such a point that he utilizes robot type gestures. Instead the movements should relate to the tone of the verbal message. An emotional point should be accompanied with an emotional gesture.

Finally, relate your gestures to the size of the audience. Larger, more pronounced gestures for auditorium style presentations. Smaller, more subtle gestures in intimate settings with smaller groups. Take a tip from the performers on Broadway, and "play to the back row".

Body Movement

Related to, but different from, gestures are the visual signals created through body movement. These signals can, in a very real sense, help in communicating your message to the audience. We have all endured presenters who tend to hide behind the podium, or stay "frozen" to one spot. We have also experienced those presenters who seem to pace back and forth like a caged lion waiting for their next meal. In both cases the movement of the presenter did little, or nothing, to enhance their presentation. Body movement can be a strong visual signal to the audience, when used in a planned, purposeful, controlled manner.

Movement gives energy to a presentation, and keeps the listener's attention focused on the speaker. Use body movement to establish contact with the listeners. Coming out from behind the podium and approaching the audience can be a very powerful tool in establishing rapport. It indicates an openness and willingness on the part of the presenter to "share" ideas. It also indicates that the presenter is at "ease" with himself, the audience, and the subject matter being presented.

Body Movement can also be used as a means of impacting the verbal message being presented. Moving from one end of the stage to another is an excellent way to indicate a change in topic. It is also very effective to move closer to the audience when making a particularly important point. Finally, if you're using visual aids, such as a flip chart, and have moved away from the easel, use body movement back to the chart as a way of focusing the audience's attention back to the point that you're trying to make.

Two important considerations regarding body movement. First, make sure that the movement is used purposefully. Avoid "wandering" or pacing, which may be distracting to the audience. Second, remember to maintain eye contact with the audience while you move, this gives the movement more impact.

Posture

How you stand provides yet another non-verbal clue to the audience. Does it support or detract from your verbal message? Your posture should be relaxed, with your hands either hanging at your sides or being used for gestures. Face the listeners head-on, shoulders square, and leaning slightly forward. Avoid unnecessary movement such as rocking back and forth, or side to side, which can be distracting to the audience. It is generally accepted that a presenter remain standing even though a speaker's stool may have been provided. There are a couple of possible exceptions to the "standing" rule, however. One is when you are speaking for a considerably long period of time. During my years as a technical instructor, when I found myself speaking for 6 to 8 hours at a time, I often sat on top of my desk for short stints. When I did however, it was purposeful and planned. Just as with body movement, the mere act of sitting was designed to convey a particular signal that enhanced the verbal message I was giving. Another case where sitting may be called for is in an informal setting when you're presenting to one or possibly two people. Sitting can put you on the same level as the listener, making your presentation more a "meeting of the minds" than an actual speech.

Appearance

Like it or not, appearance is important. In fact, it is the key ingredient in creating that all-important first impression. Our appearance is the first thing the audience notices, even before we get up to speak. If we all looked like actor Robert Redford or supermodel Christy Brinkley, then we could probably create a positive first impression just by showing up. Unfortunately many of us are not so gifted. We have to work to insure that the first impressions we create are favorable to the audience. We need our visual appearance to provide a strong visual statement to the audience of who we are.

Of all the factors that influence our appearance, none is more important than how we dress. Our clothes provide a "self portrait", communicating to the audience who we are, and what we think of ourselves. It is important that what we wear contribute to the perceptions that we want to create with the audience. Having spent most of my life in the computer industry, I have seen all sorts of presenters, in all sorts of outfits. It is not uncommon to see highly technical presenters, particularly those in the programming profession, tend to dress "down", even to the point of wearing blue jeans and sandals, while delivering a speech to their peers. At the same time, other presenters, delivering their talks to audiences with more of a marketing orientation, are more inclined to dress "up" in three piece suits and wing-tip shoes. Each type of presenter can be very effective with their respective audiences. Each uses his clothing to help create the perception they want. As you can surmise, the key to proper dress is in knowing your audience and it's expectations.

Clothing should be used to add to your message, not detract from it. Men who wear ties or shirts that consist of bright colors or patterns, as well as women who wear jewelry that dangles or makes noise, run the risk of having the listener focus their attention away from the verbal message. The most appropriate dress should accomplish its purpose, yet not be memorable to the listener.

CHAPTER 4

DOs & DON'Ts
FOR AN EFFECTIVE
DELIVERY

This chapter takes a light-hearted look at some of the more important factors influencing the effectiveness of a presentation. They are:

"DOs & DON'Ts"
IN DELIVERING A
PRESENTATION

1. <u>DO</u> Be Natural

2. <u>DON'T</u> Forget To Use Eye Contact

3. <u>DO</u> Know Your Audience

4. <u>DON'T</u> Just Read Your Speech

5. <u>DO</u> Know Your Material

6. <u>DO</u> Be Prepared

7. <u>DON'T</u> Verbalize Pauses

8. <u>DO</u> Respect The Schedule

#1 DO - BE NATURAL

The non-verbal signals we provide during the presentation must be a natural extension of ourselves. A speaker should avoid any attempt to use gestures, facial expressions, or vocal mannerisms that are not a normal part of his own particular behavior pattern. I have seen many speakers, like our friend up above who seem to "orchestrate" their presentations by incorporating gestures and movements that are not consistent with either their personalities, or the verbal message they are trying to convey. These gestures invariably come off looking phony, and the presentation suffers because of it. Everyone has their own natural individual mannerisms that they use in conversation, the trick is to use these very same mannerisms as part of the presentation. When you speak you should be genuine. Be yourself, and the audience will come away from the presentation with the feeling that you "believe" in what you're presenting.

> **Notable Quote:**
> *"All faults may be forgiven of him who has perfect candor".*
> -Walt Whitman

#2 DON'T - UNDERESTIMATE EYE CONTACT

Do not underestimate the importance of eye contact. Of all the non-verbal ways in which we communicate, the eyes are the most important. An effective presentation is a collaborative effort between you (the presenter) and the audience. This collaborative effort involves a two-way communication process that is primarily transmitted through eye contact. If you don't establish and maintain eye contact with the audience, then you're not making them a part of the presentation, and the communication process will break down. Eye contact to used to "draw" the audience into the presentation. Eye contact with a listener, says, "I'm talking to *you*", and "*you* are important to me". Eye contact also allows you to see how the audience is responding to your verbal message. As you look around the room you can monitor each listener's responses and adjust your message accordingly. Does the audience look confused? Bored? Or do they instead, look totally engaged in the communication process.

Notable Quote:
"When the eyes say one thing and the tongue another, a practiced man relies on the language of the first".
- Ralph Waldo Emerson

#3 DO - KNOW YOUR AUDIENCE

Don't be like our speaker above. When you are called upon to speak to a group that you may not be familiar with, make sure that you do your homework. A good presenter insures that he knows who he's speaking to, the purpose of the meeting, and the needs of the organization; and then formulates his message accordingly. Even if you're presenting within your own company, it is necessary to insure that you have some idea who will be in the audience. The way you present to management may be considerably different than the way you present to your peers or subordinates. You may end up delivering the same message, but you will probably need to present that message in a different way. Remember when you are delivering your message, managers are typically more bottom-line oriented, technical people get excited over facts and data, while salespeople are more likely to be wondering what's in it for them. An effective presentation takes into consideration the desires and expectations of the audience.

> **Notable Quote:**
> *"Learning is the property of those who fear to do disagreeable things".*
> -Pietro Aretino (1537)

#4 DON'T - JUST READ YOUR SPEECH

A speaker reduces his chance of successfully delivering his message by either reading a speech directly, or by reciting a memorized speech. A speech read from a manuscript is extremely difficult to deliver effectively. First of all, it leaves the presenter with few options for incorporating those all-important visual and vocal signals. Secondly, a speech that is written well, may not produce the best oral presentation. There is a considerable difference between the written word and the spoken word. Oral language typically consists of short sentences and phrases, with an inherent mixture of slang, contractions, and pauses. The written word is quite different. It consists of longer, more formal sentences that may look good on paper but ends up sounding mechanical to a listener.

Notable Quote:

"Improvisation is the essence of a good talk. Heaven defend us from the talker who doles out things prepared for us! But let heaven not less defend us from the beautifully spontaneous speaker who puts his trust in the inspiration of the moment!"

-Lytton Strachey (1946)

#5 DO - KNOW YOUR MATERIAL

The best way to enhance your delivery skills is to know your material. Once the material you're presenting has become a part of you, you can turn your attention to those non-verbal skills that can really drive your point home. Knowing your material involves a two step approach. First, know the subject matter that you are going to present. This involves research and extensive reading. Sometimes you may feel like our friend in the picture, but the effort is well worth it. The second part of knowing your material is to know your verbal message. I have seen many presenters who no doubt are experts in their field, but have no idea what points they want to make during the presentation. Only after you know the main points of the presentation, can you use non-verbal techniques to enhance those points.

Notable Quote:

"The raft of knowledge ferries the worst sinner to safety".

-**Bhagavadgita**

#6 DO - BE PREPARED

Giving a presentation is a lot like walking a tightrope. When everything is in "balance" it can actually be fun. When things start to go wrong, however, a presenter can easily find himself thinking the words: *"beam me up, Scotty "*. The difference in these two situations is preparation. Preparation, is essential to making a presentation effective, and should not be overlooked. It was Mark Twain who once acknowledged that *"it takes three weeks to prepare a good ad-lib speech"*. Being prepared means that you have thought about the presentation in advance. Not only have you considered what may go wrong, but you have also arranged for a solution just in case it does.

Preparation also builds confidence, and that confidence will be apparent to the listeners and will reflect itself in your gestures, facial expressions, and voice qualities.

> **Notable Quote:**
> *"Life is the only art that we are required to practice without preparation."*
>
> **- Lewis Mumford (1951)**

"AH. . . UM. . . . . . UH . . . YA KNOW?"

#7 DON'T - VERBALIZE PAUSES

Earlier we discussed pauses as an effective technique to convey a vocal message. There is an inherent feeling in many speakers, however, that a pause is a vacuum that has to be filled. This feeling often leads the speaker into committing one of the most unforgivable sins of public speaking. Namely, filling in these pauses with stock words or phrases. This is referred to as verbalizing the pause. A verbalized pause can be anything from a sound (ahh, uh, um, etc), to a word or phrase (ya know, like, etc) which the speaker uses to fill those gaps in his talk. A verbalized pause not only reflects negatively on the speaker's expertise, but can also be downright annoying to the audience. Just think back to the last time you heard an interview with a sports figure regarding the big game, and every three or four words were separated by a "you know". What evaluation did you make regarding his education and background.

Notable Quote:

"True eloquence consists of saying all that should be said, and that only."

　　　　　　　　　　　　-La Rochefoucauld (1665)

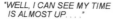

#8 DO - RESPECT THE SCHEDULE

We have all seen it. A speaker gets up to deliver a 30-minute presentation and "drones" on for what seems like hours. Not only is it an annoyance to the audience, but it is inconsiderate to any other speakers who may also be on the agenda. One of the first rules of public speaking is to adhere to the schedule. A common fear with many novice presenters involves running out of material and having nothing left to say. To counteract this fear, they tend to develop, into their presentation, more information in the form of antidotes, stories, or experiences to insure that they can "fill" their allotted time. What happens however is just the opposite, a presentation is much more likely to take more time than anticipated, not less. If you are asked to speak for 60 minutes, a good rule of thumb is to develop a presentation that goes no longer than 50 minutes. A 30-minute presentation should be prepared for 25 minutes and so on. Remember the old speaker's adage, "*Be prepared, Be sincere, Be interesting, and Be seated*".

> **Notable Quote:**
> *"Few things tend more to alienate friendship than a want of punctuality in our engagements."*
>
> - **William Hazlitt (1826)**

PART 2

THE
CONTENT

CHAPTER 5

PROVIDING EFFECTIVE CONTENT

In the first part of this book we concentrated on two key elements of what I call the **W.A.T.E.R.** process for achieving a successful presentation. These elements involved techniques for *Taking Control of Your Fear* and developing those all-essential *Effective Speaking Skills*. A complete understanding of these steps will impact the non-verbal aspects of the communication process.

Part II, of this book covers two additional elements in the **W.A.T.E.R.** process, a *Well Written Presentation* and *Audience Analysis*. These steps influence the verbal portion of the communication process referred to as the *"Content"*. The Content of a presentation goes hand-in-hand with the non-verbal signals discussed in Part 1 to effectively convey the message of the presentation to the listener.

An effective presentation is similar to dining in a fine restaurant. You want that special feeling that you get when you're treated well by the Matre De, the waiter, and even the busboy. It puts you in a good mood, and adds to your enjoyment of the meal. This is similar to the effects that the non-verbal aspects of a presentation can give. No matter how well treated you are, however, it will all go to waste if the food just doesn't *taste good*. The food in this case is the *"Content"*. A presentation must address both the verbal and non-verbal aspects of the communication process equally in order to be effective, and allow the presenter to truly *"Say More While Speaking Less"*.

This chapter takes a look at several techniques that help in determining the content of the presentation. It is a "cookbook", if you will, for providing the best food to go with the best service.

INTRODUCTION TO
VERBAL COMMUNICATION

The verbal portion of a presentation consists primarily of the words that are used to express the thoughts, ideas, and opinions of the speaker. The UCLA study, which was previously discussed in part 1, had indicated that these words create a relatively small impact (7%) on the listener. Although true, this is somewhat misleading. You see, the study took for granted that the verbal portion of the message was understandable to the listener. If this message fails to be understandable, then it will most certainly have disastrous effects on the entire presentation no matter how well the non-verbal portion of the presentation is received.

Additionally, it is up to the presenter to make sure that the verbal message itself creates an interest in the listener. Many presenters will use the non-verbal techniques discussed in part I in an attempt to establish and maintain the listener's interest, but then turn right around and lose that interest by not providing a verbal message that the listener can identify with. The verbal portion of the communication process must be written to provide the maximum effect on the audience. It is only then that the non-verbal skills can be used to their maximum advantage.

It is up to the presenter, to insure the overall effectiveness of the presentation by the choice of words that are used. Communication of the verbal message can be optimized when the presenter uses words that are designed to convey meaning in a direct, clear, and understandable manner to the listener.

KEYS TO PROVIDING EFFECTIVE CONTENT

Ask a group of professional speakers for hints on developing an effective presentation and you will probably be told to *"make it simple"*, *"make it meaningful"*, and *"make it focused"*.

GOLDEN POINT #4:

AN EFFECTIVE PRESENTATION SHOULD BE: SIMPLE, MEANINGFUL, AND FOCUSED.

Figure 5A

Ask those same speakers how to develop a *truly great* presentation and the answer will almost certainly come back, *"make it simpler"*, *"make it more meaningful"*, and *"make it even more focused"*. These are three universally accepted rules for creating a presentation with effective content. GOLDEN POINT #4 as illustrated in figure 5A emphasizes the importance of these rules.

Make it Simple

One secret to providing an outstanding verbal message is simplicity. Simplicity in the ideas we present and simplicity in the words we use to express those ideas. Lincoln's Gettysburg Address is today considered one of the best speeches of the 19th century. On the day it was delivered, however, it was not so well received. In fact, at the end of the speech much of the audience sat in stunned silence. What Abraham Lincoln actually did was create a speech that "read" well but did not "hear" well. Many in the audience could not relate to the "words" of the speech.

Unlike the Gettysburg Address, a presentation should consist of conversational words that relate directly to the listener. Each member of the audience should receive the verbal portion of the presentation as if it was the result of a one-on-one conversation with the presenter. If you are not inclined to pick the "fanciest" or the most "complex" words for use in a normal conversation, then there is no reason why you should use them as part of a presentation. Be sure to define any terms that you use which the audience may not readily understand. Avoid industry jargon unless you're sure it's understandable by the listeners. Finally, keep your use of acronyms to a minimum. Remember that an effective presentation is one in which each of the listeners feel that the speaker is relating directly to them.

Make it meaningful

Another means of enhancing your verbal message is to make it meaningful to the listener. Select words and phrases that conjure up images that the audience can relate to. This was a particular strength of former President

Ronald Reagan who was known for using the verbal portion of his message with great success. In fact, during his 1984 re-election bid, President Reagan put imagery well ahead of substance in what has often been called the "Morning in America" campaign. In this campaign, President Reagan was able to appeal to an entire electorate with statements like:

> *"How can we not believe in the greatness of America? How can we not do what is right and needed to preserve the last best hope of man, on Earth? After all our struggles to restore America, to revive confidence in our country, and hope for the future, after all our hard-won victories earned through the patience and courage of every citizen, we cannot, must not, and will not turn back. We will finish our Job."*
>
> **- Ronald Reagan**

Take a tip from Ronald Reagan, If you design your words to appeal to the listener on an emotional level, your presentation will be more interesting and more memorable because of it.

Make it focused

Recently, I attended a product presentation given to a group of salespeople. The person who gave that presentation spoke quite well. His non-verbal skills were excellent and his knowledge of the product was exceptional. He was scheduled to speak for 40 minutes but ended up speaking for an hour and a half (to me, an unforgivable sin, since I was the speaker to follow him). He began his presentation by introducing his company, defining its corporate objectives and showing some organizational charts. During his presentation, he made an effort to tell the audience everything there was to tell about his product. He went into considerable detail on how the product was designed, how it was constructed, and what enhancements were scheduled for the future. He discussed each feature of the product and how it related to the many other products his company also produced. He finished by profiling various customers who used the product and outlined each of their experiences with it. When the presenter finally sat down he seemed quite satisfied that his presentation had gone very well. Later, after the session had finished, he approached me to ask what I thought of the presentation. After careful consideration, my only response to the presenter was, *"Less would have been more"*.

The truth is, that in many speaking situations, "less *is* more". I thought the speaker had done a fine job on the delivery of the presentation. It was the "*focus*" that was missing. It appeared to me that his presentation was "audience independent". By that I mean that it was written to appeal a wide range of listeners including corporate management, system designers, engineers, users, as well as Salespeople. There was something in the presentation to appeal to everyone, including the salespeople who comprised most of the audience. The problem was that the information, which addressed the needs of the salespeople, was so diluted by the abundance of non-essential information that it lost much of it's impact. Out of the 90 minutes presented, maybe 20 minutes were appropriate to the goal of the listeners. It would have been easier on the presenter, and more effective for the audience, if the body of the presentation had contained <u>only those 20 minutes</u>.

STYLES OF PRESENTATIONS

There are four styles of presentations that are largely differentiated by the degree of advanced preparation that is given to the verbal content of the message. They are:

- Impromptu
- memorized
- Read Aloud
- Extemporaneous

Impromptu

In an Impromptu presentation the speaker is given little, if any, chance to develop a verbal message in advance. The speaker must collect his thoughts and deliver them on the spur of the moment. This style of presentation is used most frequently in business meetings, where a participant may be asked to comment on a particular point or as part of a question and answer session after a speaker has finished with the formal presentation.

An Impromptu speech can take its toll on even the most experienced of presenters. It can, without a doubt, create the highest level of anxiety of any of the presentation styles, but impromptu speaking, like anything else, is a learned art and the more you do it, the more natural it will become. To this end, Toastmaster's International, a organization devoted to enhancing presentation skills, will set aside a portion of each and every meeting for what is terms "Table Topics", where all members are required to get up and deliver a short impromptu speech. Here are some hints on surviving the ordeal of impromptu speaking:

- **Relax** - The ideas will flow much better when you're at ease.

- **Act Confident** - Your life may be flashing in front of your eyes but there's no reason that the audience should know that.

- **Be Brief** - When you're asked to speak on a subject, get up and talk about that specific point and then sit down. A single well thought out comment, expressed in less than 60 seconds, can make an outstanding impression.

- **Stick To Your Background and Experience** - If you must provide additional data, expand on your remarks by using subject matter that you are personally familiar with. In many cases you can even alter the subject to suit your own particular knowledge. Take a lesson from the football player in the following story:

Some years back, at William's College, there was a class entitled "Survey of the New Testament". This class was a particular favorite of the football team. Not because they were following some divine impulse to be called into the service of God, but because the professor, a retired Episcopal Minister always gave the same final examination each year: "<u>Trace and Delineate the Travels of the Apostle Paul</u>". This meant that they, and the rest of the class, could cut class with impunity, secure in the knowledge that they could face the final examination question on the travels of the Apostle Paul.

In one year, the good minister shocked the class by writing on the blackboard for the final exam: "<u>Analyze and Criticize the Sermon On The Mount</u>". The class was stunned, especially the football players who scratched their heads and searched for words. That is, all but one lineman who was not particularly bright, he wrote for the whole period.

When the tests were returned he had a B+, and the highest grade it the class. His paper began something like this:

"Who am I to criticize the words of the Master? Instead, I would like to discuss the travels of the Apostle Paul. . . . . ."

Some final words about impromptu speaking . . . .It is rarely impromptu. A good speaker will have anticipated the subject matter, and have conceived several ideas in advance. So the next time you marvel at some speaker's ability to provide a dynamic talk on an impromptu basis, remember, it was Mark Twain who first remarked that *"It took three weeks to prepare a good ad-lib speech"*.

Read aloud

On the other end of the style spectrum is a presentation that is read aloud. This certainly eliminates the problem of *"what to say"* which exists with an impromptu speech, but it clearly creates a whole new set of problems all it's own. A presentation that is read directly from a manuscript is difficult to deliver effectively. First of all, you will almost always sacrifice some of the freshness and spontaneity necessary to hold an audience's attention. Secondly, reading aloud limits many of the vocal and visual techniques that are part of the all important non-verbal communication process.

Although I strongly recommend against anyone presenting in this format, there are occasions where it does become necessary. Politicians may have to rely on reading a speech directly, especially if it was written by one of their speechwriters. Corporate Executives may also find themselves in a situation where a speech should be read directly. This usually occurs when the importance of the presentation is such that any change in wording can create a misunderstanding or conflict, such as presentations that address their company's directions or policies. Scientists presenting their findings at a technical conference, or Heads-of-State outlining policy decisions, may also decide to read their presentations for this same reason.

If you should find yourself in a situation where you must read aloud, there are some simple techniques that you can use to increase its effectiveness:

- **Create a Readable Manuscript** - If you must read your speech directly, at least make it easy on yourself. Create a manuscript that can be read without any difficulty. Type the speech in capital letters, using double spacing between each line and triple spacing between each paragraph. Use wide margins and leave at least 3 inches blank at the bottom of each page. This will keep your eyes focused toward the middle of the page.

- **Practice With The Actual Manuscript** - When you rehearse your speech, read from the actual script you will be using during the presentation.

- **Maintain Eye Contact With The Audience** - Eye contact can make a significant difference in how well your presentation is received by the audience, especially while reading aloud. Good eye contact is necessary to validate the audience and let them know you are talking *to them* not *at them*. Look up often and establish eye contact while reading, particularly during the last part of each sentence or paragraph. Remember, proper eye contact will insure that your points create a greater impact on the audience. Many presenters are worried that they might lose their place while looking up from the script, if this is you, do what the professionals do, move your thumb along the outside margin of your manuscript as you read. Then after you look up, all you have to do is use your thumb to establish where you've left off.

Memorized

When I think of a speaker who is considering whether or not to deliver a memorized speech I tend to recall the famous quote used by the Clint Eastwood character in the movie "Dirty Harry". As Harry stands over a suspect who is considering whether or not to reach for his own gun, Harry says:

> *"I know what your thinking, 'did he fire six shots or was it only five'? Well in all the excitement, I kinda lost track myself. But since this gun is a 44 magnum, the most powerful handgun on the face of the Earth, you've got to ask yourself one question, 'Do I feel lucky?'....*
>
> *....Well, do ya punk?"*

First the good news, the memorized speech, when carried out flawlessly, can be an outstanding method of presenting. It provides the same accurate content that exists with a speech that is read aloud, while at the same time allowing the presenter the flexibility of providing the non-verbal signals necessary to make the presentation a total success.

Now for the bad news, although some of my best presentations have been prepared so well that they, in fact, became memorized, I strongly suggest against the use of such a style. The consequences of unintentionally altering the verbal message or "drawing a blank" are just too great. Even on those occasions when I personally felt that I knew every word cold, I still carried an outline to the podium. Like a tightrope walker that uses a net, I made sure I had something to fall back on.

Another problem with the memorized style of delivery is that it leaves the presenter with little option to edit the presentation while it is being given. As was mentioned in Part 1, a presentation is a collaborative effort between the listener and the speaker. Many times a speaker will decide to alter his presentation as a result of the feedback he is receiving from the audience. Additionally, it is likely that a speaker will be asked to lengthen or shorten the presentation due to a change of the agenda or a scheduling problem. A presenter must then attempt to edit the presentation to satisfy these time constraints. In either case, the editing of a memorized presentation is extremely difficult and can cause the speaker a significant amount of stress.

Whenever you're considering giving a memorized presentation, remember the words uttered by Clint Eastwood, and ask yourself:

"Do I feel lucky?". . . .

. . . . .Well do ya?

Extemporaneous

An excellent compromise between the impromptu presentation and one that is read or memorized is the extemporaneous presentation. An Extemporaneous presentation is one in which the presenter has time to carefully formulate the verbal message of the presentation in advance.

Extemporaneous presentations allow the speaker to do detailed planning, prepare an outline or notes in which to speak from, and practice the verbal message. This tends to be the presentation style most often used by presenters.

SUMMARY OF PRESENTATION STYLES

The tables shown below and on the following page summarize the key factors that are involved in each of the previously discussed presentation styles. It should be noted that all of these styles have their own distinct advantages and disadvantages. The presenter will usually find that the situation will most likely dictate which of the above styles would be most appropriate.

For purposes of this book, however, we will assume the presentation to be of the Extemporaneous style with particular attention paid to the Planning, Preparing and Practicing of this style of presentation.

SUMMARY OF PRESENTATION STYLES

DESCRIPTION:

IMPROMPTU	READ ALOUD	MEMORIZED	EXTEMPOR - ANEOUS
• "Off the Cuff"	• Read Directly From Script	• Recited Directly From Memory	• Planned
• No Preparation			• Prepared
• High Stress			• Practiced

SITUATION:

IMPROMPTU	READ ALOUD	MEMORIZED	EXTEMPOR - ANEOUS
• Meetings • Interviews • Q&A Sessions	• Political talks • Scientific Seminars • Policy statements • Religious Services	• Rarely used • Stage Acting	• Most speaking occasions

ADVANTAGE:

IMPROMPTU	READ ALOUD	MEMORIZED	EXTEMPOR - ANEOUS
The message will usually carry a greater impact.	Accurate reflection of verbal content.	Accurate verbal content with the ability to use non-verbal signals	Allows the presenter to formulate the message in advance

DISADVANTAGE

IMPROMPTU	READ ALOUD	MEMORIZED	EXTEMPOR - ANEOUS
No time to prepare and extremely stressful	Lack of non-verbal signals to keep the presentation alive and interesting	Inflexible and has a high probability of failure	Tends to lack some of the spontaneity of the Impromptu presentation

WRITING THE PRESENTATION

Regardless of which presentation style a speaker intends on using, the actual writing of the presentation remains the same. It begins with an idea in the mind of the speaker. This idea may be as simple as a minor point the presenter wishes to make, or as complex as the complete plans for a new product offering. The writing of the presentation consists of committing this idea to paper, then developing and expanding upon this idea until it becomes a verbal message that will accurately convey the presenter's idea to the listener.

Sometimes the writing of a presentation may seem an overwhelming task to perform. The presenter may find himself asking, "How do I start?" "What information should I include?" How will I know when I'm done? The developing of a presentation is really quite simple if you follow the four "P's" of writing a presentation that is illustrated in figure 5B.

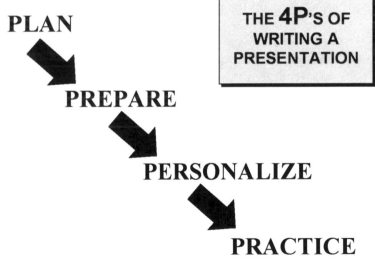

PLAN

PREPARE

PERSONALIZE

PRACTICE

THE **4P's** OF WRITING A PRESENTATION

Figure 5B

The following chapters will break down each of these activities into a step by step process and discuss several tools that will enable you, the presenter, to quickly take your idea and formulate it into a successful presentation.

Chapter 6

Planning The Presentation

An effective presentation is the result of much more than just a well executed delivery, it requires planning. Planning, more than any single item can directly impact the success of a presentation. Regardless of the subject matter to be presented, or the style of the delivery, one thing remains constant, the more effectively a presentation is planned, the better it will be received by the audience.

Planning a presentation is not unlike preparing for a trip. Try to think of the last time that you took a major vacation. What items were planned ahead of time, and what items were merely left to chance? It is almost certain than you would not leave for a vacation unless you knew *where* you were going, *how* you were going to get there, and *what* activities you would be engaged in while you were there. Careful planning of a trip would also include knowing *when* you would leave, and *how long* you would be gone. To a lesser degree, some thought would also have to be given to which clothes were appropriate, what items needed to be brought (cameras, suntan lotion, passport, etc.), and what kind of people you would be in contact with (language, local customs, etc.). Whether it's a week-long skiing trip to Europe, or just a trip to your favorite family member's house for the afternoon, the success of that trip will rely on the advanced planning that is done.

While I'll be the first to admit that delivering a presentation is "*no vacation*", the same planning and attention to detail is necessary to insure it's success. This planning process consists of the six simple steps outlined in figure 6A, which amount to nothing more than the same basic *Who?*, *What?*, *When?*, *Where?*, *Why* process which was previously used in the vacation scenario.

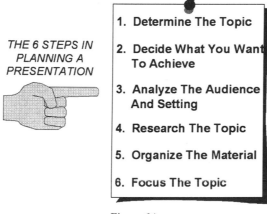

THE 6 STEPS IN
PLANNING A
PRESENTATION

1. Determine The Topic

2. Decide What You Want To Achieve

3. Analyze The Audience And Setting

4. Research The Topic

5. Organize The Material

6. Focus The Topic

Figure 6A

STEP 1:
DETERMINE THE TOPIC

In many speaking occasions the topic of the presentation will be determined, at least in part, by the group which you were invited to address or the situation surrounding your talk. A speaker, for example, addressing a public hearing, gathered to consider the building of a new community swimming pool, is not likely to discuss the pro's and con's of gun control. Instead, the speaker is expected to voice an opinion for or against the swimming pool and explain why.

In a business environment it is also very common that a presenter will be asked to speak to a specific topic. This is because, in most business meetings, the subject to be discussed is determined prior to the meeting and the participants including the speaker are selected to add value to that subject.

Does this mean that in either of these situations, we can skip step #1? Probably not! Even though a subject may have been selected in advance, we still may have to determine which aspect of that subject we are going to present. In the case of the new swimming pool, for example, we may address the financial impacts of a new swimming pool, or maybe its affects on the surrounding community.

There are, however, many speaking occasions, such as the infamous "after-dinner" speech, where the topic will often be left up to the speaker. In these situations the selection of a topic becomes the initial step in the planning process of the presentation. The selection of a topic, not only has obvious importance in the development of the presentation, it also has a significant impact on how well the presentation is received by the audience. To provide the best chance for a successful presentation it is important that the speaker select a subject that meets at least two criteria.

First, the topic selected for the presentation must be one in which the speaker has some expertise. Presenters should never pick a topic that does not directly relate to their own personal knowledge and/or experiences. It is a rare speaker who can give a convincing talk on a subject he knows little about.

The second criteria requires that the selected topic be of interest to both the speaker and the audience. It is easy to understand why the topic must be interesting to the audience. Without that interest in the topic it would be difficult to achieve and maintain the attention of each listener. It is just as important, however, that the topic also be interesting to the speaker. A speaker who lacks interest in the subject of the presentation cannot be expected to make that subject interesting to the audience. Many a well-prepared presentation has fallen "flat" because the speaker was not excited about the topic.

STEP 2:
DECIDE WHAT YOU WANT TO ACHIEVE

Once a speaker has decided on *"what"* to talk about, the next question that must be faced is *"why?"*. The leading cause of poor presentations are speakers who begin by asking *"what am I going to say?"*, instead of, *"what do I want to achieve?"*. Trying to plan a presentation without knowing what you want to achieve sort of reminds me of the following exchange between Alice and the Cheshire Cat:

Said Alice to the Cheshire Cat, "Would you tell me please, which way I ought to walk from here?"

"That depends a good deal on where you want to get to," said the Cat.

"I don't care where -----" said Alice.

"Then it doesn't matter which way you walk," said the Cat.

"------As long as I get somewhere," Alice added as an explanation.

"Oh, you're sure to do that," said the Cat, "If you only walk long enough."

-Alice's Adventures In Wonderland
by Lewis Carroll

Many speakers find themselves in a similar situation as Alice. They believe that they will *get* somewhere if, to paraphrase the Cheshire Cat, they only *talk* long enough. You can usually spot this type of presentation, it lacks a "sense of purpose". The speaker will generally fill time by providing a deluge of facts associated with a particular subject. The problem with these "facts based" presentations is that they usually fail to address either the needs of the speaker or the needs of the audience. In my career I have seen hundreds of "sales" presentations which never got around to "selling". Instead they amounted to nothing more than a "fact sheet" for the product. Determining in advance what it is that you want to achieve with the presentation can eliminate this problem.

Determining what it is that you want to achieve prior to the preparation of the presentation, is by far the most important part of the planning process. It provides a "road map" that gives the presenter a chance to focus that planning around the objective of the presentation. Allowing the presenter to maximize the effectiveness of the presentation. This also happens to be GOLDEN POINT #5.

GOLDEN POINT #5:

DETERMINE WHAT YOU WANT TO ACHIEVE PRIOR TO PREPARING THE PRESENTATION

Figure 6B

A 20-minute presentation is more than just 20 minutes of presenting. Each and every presentation should be viewed as an opportunity for the speaker to accomplish a desired objective. It is this objective that answers the question "*What do I want to achieve?*" Every presentation must have an objective. If you find yourself preparing for a presentation in which there is no apparent objective or where there is nothing significant to be achieved, you should "run for the hills". This is probably a presentation that shouldn't be given at all.

When preparing a presentation, there are two forms that the objective should take. The *General Objective* and the *Specific Objective*.

General Objective

The *General Objective* represents the presentation's overall purpose. It's the reason for giving the presentation in the first place. Typically the general objective of a presentation will fall into one or more of the following categories:

- **To Inform or Instruct** - If the goal of the speaker is to help the members of the audience comprehend an idea or process, then the general objective is considered to be to inform or instruct. In this type of presentation the speaker seeks to widen the range of the audience's knowledge by providing facts that are typically new to the listener. Presentations of this type represent a vast majority of all presentation given today. To inform or instruct an audience can take place anywhere from the classroom to the boardroom.

- **To Persuade or Sell** - If the goal of the speaker is to influence the listener's beliefs or feelings, then the general objective is to persuade or sell. In theory persuading or selling involves considerably more strategy than informing. Informing typically consists of supplying new information, while persuading involves overcoming the resistance of other ideas or old habits. Whether the goal involves the selling of ideas, or a specific product, it is imperative that the speaker clearly express a viewpoint and use the presentation to support that viewpoint. In a presentation designed to persuade or sell, there should never be any doubt on the part of the listener what the speaker is attempting to prove.

- **To Inspire or Initiate Action** - If the goal of the speaker is to create a desire in the audience to move ahead with a proposed solution, then the general objective is to inspire or initiate action. Unlike persuading, inspiring action does not usually require the altering of the listener's beliefs. Instead, it is the act of reinforcing and intensifying feelings that are already resident in the listener. Knute Rockne's stirring "win one for the Gipper" speech could never have inspired the Notre Dame football team to overcome a 34-0 half-time deficit and defeat Army, unless each of his players already had the common desire to win. Don't look for many "facts" in a presentation that is designed to inspire or initiate action, they won't be there. Its effectiveness is directly related to the speaker bypassing the "head" of the listener and going directly to the "heart".

- **To Entertain** - If the goal of the speaker is primarily to amuse the audience, then the general objective is to entertain. A presentation that entertains is designed to place the audience in a specific mood. Humor is the most common, but not the only tool used in these types of presentations. Stories, personal experiences, and observations can all be used quite effectively to entertain an audience.

Specific Objective

To complement the general objective, there is a second, more definitive, form that the presentation's objective takes. This is referred to as the *Specific Objective*. The specific objective represents the central theme that links together all the ideas of the presentation, and provides the basis for the actual verbal message that the presenter wishes to convey. A speaker may, for example, give a presentation in which listeners are instructed (*General Objective*) on the proper of care and feeding of animals (*Specific Objective*). It is the details of animal care and feeding that make up the specific objectives.

The Specific Objective further defines the General Objective by stating "what" it is that you want to accomplish with the presentation. In its simplest form a Specific Objective may be the completion of the following statements:

General Objective	Specific Objective
Inform/ **Instruct**	When I finish the presentation I would like the audience to ***know*** _____
Persuade/ **Sell**	When I finish the presentation I would like the audience to ***feel*** _____
Inspire/ **Initiate Action**	When I finish the presentation I would like the audience to ***want*** _____
Entertain	When I finish the presentation I would like the audience to ***be*** _____

Establishing both the general objective and the specific objectives can provide the presenter with "guideposts" to help in the development of the presentation. The general objective for example, helps the presenter with questions involving format and organization. While the specific objective is used by the presenter to focus the topic, and to help in determining which information is necessary to insure that the presentation achieves it's goals.

STEP 3:
ANALYZE THE AUDIENCE AND SETTING

An effective presentation requires a speaker, a listener, and a message that passes between them. All too often while planning a presentation, the viewpoint of the listener is overlooked. Speakers may become so engrossed in their own interests and so impressed by the ideas that seem important to them, that they forget that they are communicating with people whose attitudes and interests may be quite different from their own. One common trait of all effective presenters is the ability to alter the presentation so that it "relates" well with the experiences of the audience. Nowhere is this ability more apparent than in a classroom setting, where the major difference between a truly outstanding teacher and one who just seems to go through the motions, is related to their ability to "see" the message from the standpoint of the listener.

Let's suppose, for example, you are asked to give a presentation on "*The American Dream*". You are told that you must give this presentation to three separate groups. One group consists of a class of high school seniors, another group is made up largely of recent immigrants to the U.S., and the third group is a luncheon gathering of local entrepreneurs. While your objectives in all three cases may indeed remain the same, it is highly unlikely that you could deliver the same verbal message to each group and get away with it. Each group may, in fact, have it's own distinct definition of what the "American dream" actually is. If this definition is not taken into account, the audience may have considerable trouble relating to the points made in your presentation. Your credibility as a speaker in each situation will depend largely on your ability to "tailor" your message so that it relates directly to the ideas and attitudes of each individual group. Proper planning for a presentation requires that you know as much as possible about the audience. To analyze the audience, your consideration may include, but not necessarily be limited to the following items, which may have a direct "*B.E.A.R.I.N.G.*" on the listener's attitudes.

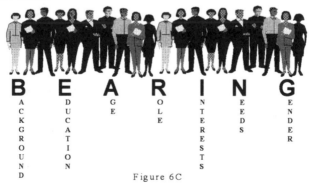

B	E	A	R	I	N	G
A	D	G	O	N	E	E
C	U	E	L	T	E	N
K	C	E	E	E	D	D
G	A			R	S	E
R	T			E		R
O	I			S		
U	O			T		
N	N			S		
D						

Figure 6C

Background	What is the background of the audience, as it relates to the topic of the presentation? Are they already knowledgeable or novices to the subject matter. A presentation should be planned so that it addresses the audience's level of knowledge.
Education	A presentation should insure that it utilizes materials, examples, and stories that are suitable to the educational experience of the audience. Make an attempt to target the presentation so that it's understandable to the average listener.
Age	Young, old, or middle aged, consider the age and experience level of the audience while planning the presentation. Which would mean more to the audience, a quote from Harry Truman or a quote from Stephen Spielberg.
Role	Consider the role that each listener has in the presentation. Are they there as part of a group, or as an individual representative of their company? A presentation should address the role that the listeners may find themselves in.
Interests	Plan a presentation so that it incorporates stories and examples that address any common interests of the audience. A football analogy may be quite appropriate at a sports banquet but not at a meeting of the league of woman voters.
Needs	Why is the audience there, and what do they hope to get out of the presentation? The audience's needs must be planned for in advance, otherwise the speaker runs the risk of failing to meet the objectives of the presentation.
Gender	Is the audience all male, all female, or mixed? The fact is that men and women both have interests and experience that are unique to their sex. Use those experiences to illustrate the key points within the presentation.

While analyzing the audience is essential, the setting in which the presentation is to occur is also an important consideration. During the planning process, a speaker should take time to insure that the presentation is developed in such a way that it takes into consideration physical elements such as the time and place of the presentation.

Some of the more important facts that should be addressed are:

- Type of room
- Size of the audience
- Seating arrangements
- Available audio/visual equipment
- Time of presentation

STEP 4:
RESEARCH THE TOPIC

Good speeches are not composed of "hot air" and generalizations. They need strong supporting materials to bolster the speaker's point of view. The success of any presentation is directly related to how well prepared the speaker is, and research is one of the keys to that preparation. The next step in the planning process involves researching the topic and gathering the necessary information to augment the presentation's verbal message. How to go about this research is the question.

First of all, it's a fact that a speaker will speak best about subjects in which there is already a familiarity. Research should therefore always begin by bringing together the facts that you already know. Combining this information with experiences and personal stories is certain to add value to any presentation. You may not have all the information, but you will probably have enough to get a good start.

When it becomes necessary to gather additional information in the form of facts, illustrations, quotes, and examples some outside research will certainly be required. This research can be done in a variety of ways. The library can be the center of much of this research. Books, magazines, newspapers, and reference materials such as encyclopedias are immediately available just for the asking. There are fast and easy ways to find whatever you want from the local library. In today's libraries those clumsy old card catalogs have, for the most part, been replaced by computerized terminals which make searching for specific data a snap.

Learn to use these terminals to locate specific titles, authors, and subjects and your research will be faster and more efficient because of it. One thing that has remained the same in today's library however, is the librarian. Librarians can be of enormous help, so if you have a question, don't hesitate to ask one.

In this age of technology even the research of information is changing at a record pace. An abundance of information services can be accessed through the use of personal computers and a modem. The *Internet* is one of these information services. Through the *Internet,* a computer can access government services including the library of congress, as well as many educational institutions throughout the world. In addition to the *Internet* are a variety of computer services such as CompuServ, America On-line, and Prodigy that also provide similar access to information.

Another method of acquiring information is through conversations and interviews with people who have a special knowledge on a particular subject. This is a time-honored way to collect information. Just ask any journalist about the importance of interviewing as a means of gathering information. Besides the wealth of information that an interview can provide, it can also lend a degree credibility to the speaker when, in the course of the presentation, it is mentioned that certain facts presented came as a result of a one on one conversation.

And finally, don't overlook the contribution that radio and television broadcasts can make in providing relevant information. Both PBS and CSPAN provide lectures, discussions and formal public addresses by leaders in government, business, education, and religion. CNN and the major entertainment networks provide news programming and interview shows such as "Crossfire", "Meet the Press" or "Face the Nation". All of these programs can be made available in transcript form for a small fee.

STEP 5:
ORGANIZE THE MATERIAL

If you're like me, you've finished up your researching of the topic with a considerable amount of notes. You probably have ended up with items written in a notebook, quotations written on scraps of paper, xerox copies of passages from books or magazines, and maybe even some facts and figures written down on the backs of envelopes. Now it's time to consolidate this information into some usable form so that it can be used in the development of the presentation.

Organizing this material is an individual process. Speakers use whatever works best for them. I for example, like to enter much of my data into a word processor so that I can "cut" and "paste" the information as I see fit. Some other speakers may prefer to enter the data on 3X5 index cards so that they can be "shuffled" and rearranged at will. Many times these index cards are tacked up on a bulletin board in sort of a "story board" format. Regardless of the organization method, the important thing is to put the information in a format that allows easy access to it as needed.

Organizing the material also gives the speaker a chance to edit the data that had been accumulated. Not all the information you've collected will be used in the presentation. Only the supporting materials that have a direct bearing on the objective should be used and anything else rejected. Speakers must be careful to avoid the impulse to add as much of these supporting material as possible. It only will dilute the information that is presented in direct support of the objectives. Remember the rules from Chapter 5 on a presentation's content - keep it simple, keep it meaningful, and keep it focused. In fact, this leads to the final planning step.

STEP 6:
FOCUS THE TOPIC

This may seem a strange step in the planning process, but I assure you it's a necessary one. We began the planning process by selecting the topic, we end it by rethinking that topic, and trying to narrow its scope. In order for a presentation to be successful, it must be focused. Good speakers want their presentation to be more like a "rifle shot" instead of a cannon. Good speakers shoot for the bullseye instead of just trying to blow up the target.

The focusing of the topic is an ongoing process. The presenter should always be looking for an opportunity to narrow the topic. Take the previous example of developing a presentation with a topic of "*The American Dream*". We go through each of the steps in the planning process. We've decided on what we want to accomplish, we've analyzed the audience and the setting, we've done the necessary research and organized the materials. At each step along the way we've obtained valuable information which can help us to focus the topic of the presentation.

Follow the chart below as this information begins to lead the presenter to a more focused topic.

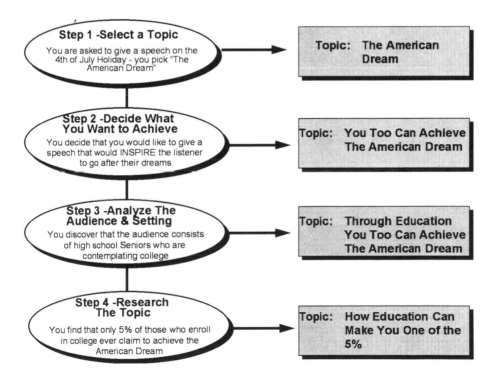

We've taken the "cannon shot" of *Achieving the American Dream* and made it a "rifle shot" that will allow the presentation to create more of an impact.

CHAPTER 7

PREPARING THE PRESENTATION

Have you ever watched a movie being made? The actual filming of a movie can be an extremely boring process. It involves the filming of many short scenes separated by long periods of apparent inactivity. What many people find most surprising though, is that these scenes are not necessarily filmed in the order that they are expected to appear in the movie. Instead, scenes are filmed in a sequence designed to make maximum use of the location, the scenery, and the actors. It is not out of the question for the ending of a movie to, in fact, be one of the very first scenes to be filmed. When filming is concluded, a movie rarely has any form or direction to it. Instead it consists of little more than a large collection of film "clips". Clips which individually mean nothing, but when combined together, in the right order, form the basis of a feature length movie. It's the film's Director and his editing team who are given the responsibility for taking these individual clips and turning them into a "work of art". In order to do this, the Director carefully examines each clip, deciding which ones are to be used in the movie, and which are to be left on the "cutting room floor". The Director then takes the surviving film clips and arranges them in an order so that they make sense, and tells the story that the Director wishes to tell. It is at this point that we can actually say that the film is prepared.

Preparing a presentation is very much like being the Director of a movie. After the planning of the presentation, you will be left with many pieces of data. This data may consist of the key points that you would like to express, facts and figures that were researched to prove those points, as well as stories and quotations that can be used to drive those points home. Like the Director, it will be necessary to edit this data and arrange it so that it makes sense. It is at this point that we can actually say that the presentation is prepared.

PRESENTATION FORMAT

The formal structure of a presentation has probably not changed much since that very first caveman got up in front of the campfire in an attempt to express an idea to the rest of the tribe. Tens of thousands of years of evolution have failed to improve on the basic three-part format:

- Opening/Introduction
- Body
- Closing/Summary

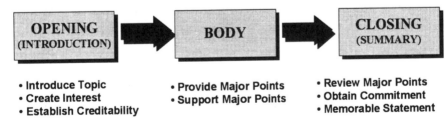

Figure 7A

This was probably summed up best by the teacher of my very first speech class when he said: *Tell them what you're going to tell them* (Opening), *tell them* (Body), and then *tell them what you told them* (Closing).

Each one of these parts provides an important function within the presentation. In order to effectively develop a presentation it is necessary to understand these functions and try to maximize their impact.

The Opening

The opening (or introduction) is extremely important to a presentation's success. It is used to accomplish three objectives. The first objective is to introduce the topic and the purpose of the presentation. The second objective is to create an interest in the audience. The last objective is to identify yourself as a speaker and establish your creditability. If there is any truth to the adage, "*You never get a second chance to make a first impression*", then you can understand the importance of accomplishing all three objectives during the opening of the presentation.

The Body

The body of the presentation contains the verbal message that you, the speaker, want to provide to the audience. The goal of the body is simply to accomplish the purpose of the presentation. Whether that purpose is to inform, persuade, inspire, or entertain, it is the body that must, not only provide, but also support the presentation's major points.

The Closing

The closing (or summary) portion of the presentation provides the listener with a review of the major points contained in the body, but that's not its primary goal. The purpose of the closing is to secure agreement or to get a commitment from the audience.

The preparation of a presentation involves the development of each of these three parts. As the picture below in figure 7B describes, the development of a presentation is done in the four steps.

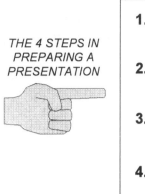

THE 4 STEPS IN PREPARING A PRESENTATION

1. **Organize The Body**

2. **Develop The Close**

3. **Develop The Opening**

4. **Develop The Body**

Figure 7B

STEP 1:
ORGANIZE THE BODY

Before the actual writing of the presentation can begin, it is necessary to create a "view" of what that presentation will ultimately look like. Much like building a house begins with the development of a blueprint, a presentation needs to begin with a plan that dictates the form and direction that the presentation will take. This plan relies on much of the work that was previously done during the Planning Phase, when the topic was selected, researched and narrowed.

Organizing the body consists of (1) Determining the main points of the presentation; (2) Phrasing these main points precisely; and (3) Arranging them strategically.

Determine the Main Points

The main points of the presentation represent the three to five key ideas that the presenter wishes to convey. Collectively, these points comprise the theme of the presentation, and form the skeleton of the body. In a vast majority of cases, the main points will be evident from the *Specific*

Objective of the presentation as determined during the Planning Process. For example, here are the main points in a recent speech given regarding the crisis in Haiti:

Haiti Policy Update

General Objective: **To inform the audience on the effects of our Haitian policy.**

Specific Objective: **To let the audience know the positive effects U.S. policy has had on the Haitian government, it's economy, and it's refugees**

Main Points:
- **U.S. policy has led to a more stable government**
- **U.S. policy has led to a stronger Haitian economy**
- **U.S. policy has decreased the flow of Haitian refugees into Florida.**

In this case the main points can be taken directly from the *Specific Objective*. If the main points are not expressly stated in the *Specific Objective,* they may still be easily projected from it. Remember, the main points of the presentation are those points that you need to make to the listeners in order to achieve the *Specific Objective*.

Phrasing the Main Points

The main points of a presentation may actually be repeated many times. Once during the opening, at least once during the body of the presentation, and again at the closing. This makes the phrasing of these points critical. The keys to proper phrasing are simplicity and consistency.

Each of the main points of the presentation must be stated simply since the success of the presentation is directly related to their being understood. State the main points as briefly as possible without distorting each point's meaning. A simple, straightforward declaration is easy for the listener to grasp; a long and complex statement tends to be vague and confusing.

It is also important that the main points be phrased consistently each and every time that they are expressed during the presentation. It will only add confusion, and hurt the presentation's overall effectiveness if a main point which was introduced as "*Competing in sports builds character*" during the opening, is then summarized as "*Competition makes you a better person*" during the closing. In addition to a consistency in referring to each main point, there should also be a consistency to the way that all the main points are phrased. Use a uniform type of sentence structure and a similar phraseology in stating each of the main points.

Arranging the Main Points

Another important consideration that must be made while organizing the body of the presentation is the order in which the main points are given. An effective presentation guides the listeners through each of the main points in an orderly sequence. This sequence should be selected so that it makes it easier for the audience to follow and remember the information. This order that you pick for the main points will also have an affect on both the clarity and persuasiveness of your ideas. These are some of the more common methods for arranging the main points of a presentation.

- **Chronological Order** - When using chronological order, the main points of the presentation are arranged based on the relative order which they occur in time. A speech given to a group of stockholders, outlining the major accomplishments of a corporation, may move through the year month by month, or quarter by quarter, listing each major accomplishment in the order that they were achieved.

- **Spatial Order** - Spatial order arranges the main points of a presentation by their physical proximity to each other. A presentation on a new design for an office building, may discuss each floor in order beginning with the main reception area, and progressing up each floor until it finishes with the executive offices in the penthouse.

- **Topical Order** - If the main points of the presentation are such that they don't lend themselves to be easily arranged by either time or space, then you might try topical order. In topical order the topic of the presentation is divided into several sub-topics that may have little connection with each other. Take the example used earlier in this chapter concerning the effects of the U.S. Haitian policy. The main points concerning government, economy, and refugees each stand on their own, but together define the topic. When using topical order, it is advantageous to present the main points in a sequence starting with the least important point and progressing to the most important point. In this manner the point of greatest significance will be the last one heard by the audience, and most likely the one that will be remembered the most.

- **Casual order** - Presentations in which all the main points can be divided into two groups - one dealing with an event and the second dealing with the effects of that event - can be grouped in casual order. Examples of casual order would involve combining the major points based on: (1) Problem/Solution, (2) Cause/Effect, and (3) Comparison/Contrast. Depending on the topic, one way of organizing these points may be to devote the first main point to a problem, with the second main point being it's solution. Another method would involve dealing with all the "problem" points first followed by all the "solution" points.

Once the body is organized, and the main points have been established and sequenced, it is time to begin the actual development of the presentation.

STEP 2:
DEVELOP THE CLOSE

Does the writing of the presentation really begin with the development of the Close? You bet! The Closing is the most critical part of the presentation. Everything done during the presentation is really done so as to support an effective close. We have all seen and heard speakers whose abrupt "Thank you" left us wondering if we had *missed something*. A speaker who fails to utilize the close to it's fullest potential cheats both himself and the audience. It is during the closing that you either accomplish your objective or you don't. In fact, the closing of the presentation is so important that, once it is developed, it should be written down and memorized. GOLDEN POINT #6 below illustrates the importance of the Close.

GOLDEN POINT #6:

THE CLOSING IS THE MOST IMPORTANT PART OF THE PRESENTATION AND SHOULD BE DEVELOPED FIRST

Figure 7C

The days when a presenter can get away with "*So in conclusion. . .*" are over. An effective close needs to accomplish the following five functions:

- Review the purpose of the presentation
- Review the main points of the presentation
- Tie the main points together
- Make a "Impact" statement
- Close should stand on it's own

Reviewing The Purpose Of The Presentation

The Closing usually begins by reiterating the presentation's purpose. In a few words or sentences the presenter should bring the listener back to why the presentation was given in the first place, and what it is that the listener should have achieved from it. This can be done easily by referring directly to the central theme of the presentation as outlined in the Opening.

Reviewing The Main Points Of The Presentation

First and foremost the closing of the presentation is there to review the main points of the presentation (remember: *"Tell them what you told them"*), and to focus the audience's attention on the importance of each point. Be careful not to spend too much time on any point during the Ending, however. If you feel the need to redefine or support a main point, it probably indicates that that point was not developed enough within the body.

Tying The Main Points Together

A good Ending should convey a sense of completeness and finality by tying the main points of the presentation together and relating them back to the purpose of the presentation. At its conclusion, the pattern established within the presentation should be brought clearly into focus for the audience.

Making An "Impact" Statement

A conclusion of a presentation should aim at leaving the audience in a receptive mood. This is done most effectively through the use of what is called an "impact" statement. Impact statements are memorable statements or quotations that reaches the listener on an "emotional" level. It should be a statement that goes to the heart of the presentation's objective, causing the listener to think about the main points of the presentation. Consider John F. Kennedy's *"...ask not what your country can do for you, but what you can do for your country"*.

Standing On It's Own

if you had just 2 minutes to tell someone the basic facts of your entire presentation what would you say? - <u>Give 'em the close!</u> The Close should be able to stand on it's own as a presentation. Having spent most of my career as a sales executive, I can't tell you the number of times I've had to use the close as my whole presentation. Believe me, in those instances where a client looks at his watch and asks you to get to the bottom line, a well developed Close comes in handy.

On the next page is a brief excerpt of the Close contained in one of President Bill Clinton's 1992 campaign speeches...... can you pick out the different aspects of the close discussed above?

We want to restore to this country a genuine sense of community and caring, to say we're all in this together. We're going up or down together, without regard to race or region or income. This is America. Let's start acting like it again.

So if you're sick and tired of the way it's been going, if you want people in control again, if you believe your country is still the greatest country in the world again, if you think we can compete and win again, if you're tired of being heartbroken when you go home at night, and you want a spring in you're step and a song in your heart, you give Al Gore and I a chance to bring America back. We will lift the country up. It's time for them to go, and time for us to rescue America.

God bless you, and God bless America. Thank you

-   Bill Clinton (7/22/92)

STEP 3:
DEVELOP THE OPENING

Once you have completed the Closing of the presentation it is time to establish an effective Opening. The benefits of a well-developed Opening cannot be overlooked. For the first 3 minutes you are an "unknown" quantity. During this time the audience will be forming their first impressions of both you and of the presentation you are beginning to deliver. Once those impressions are formed, it may well affect the way your entire presentation is received.

The overriding purpose of the Opening then, is to create these positive first impressions and to direct the audience's attention to the subject of the presentation. An effective Opening accomplishes at least three things. It must:

- Create Interest
- Establish Creditability
- Introduce the Topic

Create Interest

Back in Chapter 1, I talked about the fact that, from the audience's point of view, many of the things that make a presentation good go unnoticed. One of these things is the generation of interest within the listener. When a listener becomes interested in a presentation it is usually no accident, and although the interest of the audience must be maintained throughout the presentation it must initially be *captured* during the Opening.

There are two means by which we can gain attention and create interest with the audience. The first is by use of a *grabber* statement. The *grabber* is very similar to the "Impact Statement" discussed during the Close. It is designed to reach the listeners on an emotional level. It may consist of a posing question or providing a startling or unusual fact, which appeals to their "head", or a story or quotation designed to appeal to their "heart". Humor is another commonly used method of creating interest, but is also one of the hardest to "pull off". Beginning a presentation with a joke that falls "flat" will probably do more harm than good.

The second method of creating interest is more subtle, but much more effective. It involves giving the audience a *reason* to pay attention to what you have to say. In it's simplest terms, it is the answer to the question "What's in it for me?" A question which, whether they admit it or not, is in the back of the mind of each and every listener. Give the audience a reason to pay attention during the opening, and it will pay dividends throughout the remainder of the presentation.

Sometimes the presenter may even do both of these within the Opening. Take for example, a presenter who begins the presentation like this:

> **Did you know that only 5% of working people are able to achieve financial independence before they reach the age of sixty-five?**
>
> **Today I'm going to tell you how _you_ can become one of those 5%.**

Is there any doubt that this presenter will immediately generate interest within his audience?

Establish Creditability

In the first 60 seconds of the presentation it is essential for you to establish credibility with the audience. In many speaking occasions, particularly those in which the audience already knows you, your credibility may have already been established. This is ideal, and there is little need to spend any of that valuable "Introduction" time pontificating on your credentials. Just get on with the presentation.

All too often though, some discussion of your background will be necessary for the audience to view you as an expert on the subject of your presentation. In situations such as these, the fastest and most efficient way of establishing your credentials is to have it come directly from the person who introduces you. Never leave your introduction to chance, whenever possible write your own introduction. If this isn't possible then attempt to at least meet with the person who will introduce you so you can discuss your introduction in advance. Provide this person with the information on your background and experience that you feel impacts your presentation's topic the most.

In those rare occasions where you are forced to discuss your own background, there are a few guidelines that should be followed. First, keep it short! Your purpose should be to establish credibility, not to give a biography of your life. The more subtle you can make your points, the better. Second, focus on real world experiences and knowledge relating to your subject, instead of listing your various degrees, honors, or memberships in specific organizations. Finally, never lead off by discussing your background. The place to establish credibility is after your "grabber" statement and before you introduce the presentation's topic. Let's take the Opening used previously and expand it to include the establishment of credibility.

> **Did you know that only 5% of working people are able to achieve financial independence by the time they reach the age of sixty-five?**
>
> **Today I'm going to tell you how _you_ can become one of those 5%.**
>
> **In my over 25 years as a financial planner, I have been able to take the knowledge I've gained and apply it to clients of various income levels with considerable success.**

Introduce the Topic

The third and last function of the Opening is to introduce the topic. At it's most basic level, introducing the topic can consist of stating the subject and listing the three to five main points that will be discussed in the presentation. Although this would be a somewhat effective way to introduce the topic, it doesn't take full advantage of the opportunity that the presenter is given to "preview" his presentation. While introducing the topic, a presenter has the chance to help the audience understand the direction that the presentation will take, and the logic that will be used to get there. A good presenter will use the Introduction like a "road map" preparing the audience for the trip they will take in the body of the presentation.

Let's complete the example of the Introduction, by introducing the topic to the audience:

> **Did you know that only 5% of working people are able to achieve financial independence by the time they reach the age of sixty-five?**
>
> **Today I'm going to tell you how _you_ can become one of those 5%.**
>
> **In my over 25 years as a financial planner, I have been able to take the knowledge I've gained and apply it to clients of various income levels with considerable success.**

> *In this presentation, I will break the secret code of financial independence by discussing a three-part investment strategy traditionally overlooked, even by the most experienced investor.*
>
> *This investment strategy consists of (1) Timing your investments, (2) risk free diversification, and (3) investment liquidity.*
>
> *Understanding these concepts can help you get a lot more out of the dollars you invest and can provide ultimate entry into the 5% club.*

STEP 4:
DEVELOP THE BODY

We began preparing the presentation by determining, and then organizing, its main points. We then developed both the Closing, which gave a brief summary of the presentation, and the Opening, which was designed to gain the audience's interest and introduce the topic. Now, in the final step it's time to focus on the "meat" of the presentation, which is the body.

If you have followed the procedures outlined in the previous chapter, you will find that developing the body of the presentation is much easier than you might have imagined. The fact is, most of the work is already done. Developing the Body of the presentation is simply accomplishing your *specific objective* by using the information acquired during your *Planning* (Chapter 6) to expand on the main points which were decided upon during step 1 of the *Preparation* (Chapter 7). It is this "expansion" of the main points that will ultimately determine the presentation's effectiveness.

In the Opening the main points were introduced, in the Closing the main points were summarized, but it is in the Body where the main points are developed, clarified, and proven for the audience. To insure their overall effectiveness, each main point within the body should be accompanied with the necessary supporting data, and a transition statement to the next point

Supporting Data

Ask any good trial lawyer and they will tell you that putting together a winning case consists of much more than just making claims and generalizations, it requires evidence. Evidence that supports the main points of the case is crucial to persuading a jury. In developing an effective presentation, It is equally as important to provide this proof. Audiences, like juries, respond to points that are accompanied with strong supporting data. Supporting data is the key to making each main point both convincing and memorable.

Collecting this supporting data is the single most time consuming part of planning and preparing a presentation. Research will usually provide an abundance of information that could be used in a presentation. The key is in selecting just the right material to substantiate your key points, while maintaining the interest of the audience.

Figure 7D

As the diagram in figure 7D indicates, supporting data can come in many forms ranging from the "hard" facts contained in statistics or expert testimony, to a "softer" approach utilizing metaphors or analogies. Which type of supporting data you end up using depends a lot on the topic of the presentation and your own personal style of presenting. Look to use combinations of the following to make your main points come alive for the audience.

- **Facts / Statistics** - We live in an age of statistics. Everywhere we go we seem to be inundated with a staggering amount of facts to digest. There are so many facts and statistics available on almost every subject, that these facts have, in many ways, lost their significance. We have all seen politicians in a debate use statistics to attack the other candidate on how he has significantly *increased* government spending, only to have the that other candidate come back with just as many statistics showing how he has significantly *decreased* government spending. It sort of reminds me of the old adage, "figures lie, and liars figure". Yet, at the same time, there is no more powerful tool for persuading a listener than to back up a main point with facts and statistics.

Sometimes a single fact can be so explosive that it stands on its own and immediately provides credibility to the entire presentation. Many facts, however, need some help. A fact or statistic can have its effectiveness increased by comparing it with some other fact that is well known to the audience.

For example let's say we were giving a presentation on the climate in baseball today. In that presentation one of our main points were that salaries were too high. Here's how that point might be supported through statistics and facts:

> *Many of the problems with baseball today can be directly attributed to the fact that salaries are too high. In 1994 the average salary of a baseball player surpassed the $1 million mark for the first time in the game's history. While the last decade has provided the average worker in this country with a modest 30% gain in earning power, the major league baseball player's earnings have increased by over 400%. Is it any wonder that 19 of the 28 Major League baseball teams were unprofitable in 1993?*

- **Illustrations** - Illustrations are stories designed to enhance or clarify the meaning of your main points. In and of themselves, illustrations do not *prove* anything. What they do instead, is help the audience understand the point you're discussing, and as a result makes that point more memorable. Illustrations designed to appeal to the listener's emotions are quite effective when used as supporting data, particularly if they make that listener laugh or cry. Most U.S. Presidents have been masters in the use of imagery or illustrations to bring a point "home" to the audience. One president, Ronald Reagan earned his nickname of "the great communicator" primarily through his use of imagery in speeches.

Let's take a look at how an illustration can be used to support the main point discussed previously:

> *Many of the problems with baseball today can be directly attributed to the fact that salaries are too high. Today's millionaire players cannot relate to the player's of years gone by who played for the love of the game. It wasn't about money then, it was about pride and tradition. Many a time a young boy would venture from his home with little more than his baseball glove and a dream to one day play for a major league baseball team.*

- **Examples** - There is an old adage in the teaching profession, *"when in doubt - give an example"*. In presentations, examples help to clarify a main point or idea by reinforcing it's meaning. Examples are similar in nature to illustrations, but are designed to appeal more to the audience's intelligence, then to their emotions. Examples, while falling short of actually proving a particular point, do provide some evidence of the likelihood that a speaker's claim is true by describing a specific instance that provides confirmation of the point in question.

Use of an example to support our main point might look something like this:

> *Many of the problems with baseball today can be directly attributed to the fact that salaries are too high. Take for example the team owner's claim that the ability to pay player's salaries have created a competitive imbalance between "rich" big-city teams such as the New York Yankees, who have fat regional television markets to tap, and small-city teams such as the San Diego Padres whose local revenue opportunities are limited.*

- **Expert Testimony** - The ideas that are represented by the main points of your presentation can often be effectively supported by quoting or paraphrasing the words of another person. When the speaker cites the opinions or conclusions expressed by "experts", it is referred to as testimony. Using expert testimony is particularly important for speaker's who may not be perceived as an expert on the subject of the presentation. A young college graduate giving a lecture on quantum physics, for example, may add a certain amount of credibility to his presentation by quoting the likes of Albert Einstein or Stephen W. Hawking.

The key to expert testimony lies with the selection of the "expert". The testimony will be only as effective as the source is both credible and known to the audience. In 1980, then President Jimmy Carter learned a valuable lesson on expert testimony when, during a debate with challenger Ronald Reagan, he quoted from a conversation that his then 9-year old daughter Amy had with him regarding the importance of nuclear disarmament. Although it was intended to show that nuclear disarmament as a priority in his administration's foreign policy, it instead left the impression that the President of the United States got his ideas from children.

Here how our main point would look if it were to be supported with expert testimony:

> *Many of the problems with baseball today can be directly attributed to the fact that salaries are too high. Los Angeles Dodger pitcher, Oral Hershiser, himself one of the highest paid players in the game, worries that today's stratospheric salaries will have the effect of making it harder than it used to be to keep players around baseball after their playing days. He is quoted as saying, "Baseball will lose a lot of knowledge because players will make enough money that they will not have to stay in baseball. In the past a lot of players stayed in baseball because it was their only asset".*

- **Quotes** - A short quote is often quite effective in focusing the audience's attention on a main point within the presentation. Quotes are quite different from the expert testimony discussed previously. They are chosen not to establish credibility, but for their "snappy" verbiage and relationship to the topic. It is typically not important who said the quote, or what expertise they posses. The importance lies in the effect that the quote has on the audience. In fact, a couple of my favorite people to quote from, are baseball manager Casey Stengal and his longtime catcher Yogi Berra, not because of their expertise, but because of the way they could "butcher" the English language. Many times a well-placed quote from one of these guys can liven up an otherwise tedious presentation.

  Our main point can be supported with a well placed quote such as the one below:

> *Many of the problems with baseball today can be directly attributed to the fact that salaries are too high. I think Franklin D. Roosevelt summed it up best when he said " It is an unfortunate human failing that a full pocketbook often groans more loudly than an empty stomach".*

- **Metaphors / Similes** - Metaphors and similes are used to create a vivid picture in the mind of the listener, which can then make the presenter's ideas more concrete and meaningful. They involve expressing one idea by relating it to another, better understood idea. Metaphors are timeless figures of speech in which one idea derives its meaning by actually being expressed as if it were something else. For example, I've heard of overprotective fathers who are said to have "*tight reins*" on their children, or an irate manager who has reached his "*boiling point*". The pictures that these words convey are all that is necessary to get the point across.

Closely linked to Metaphors, are similes. A simile accomplishes the same function as a metaphor, but it does it in a slightly different way. A simile consists of a direct comparison between the speaker's idea, and one that paints a picture for the listener. I remember an old advertisement for the Sealy Mattress company that said "*Sleeping on a Sealy is like sleeping on a cloud*". I'm willing to bet none of us have ever slept on a cloud, but we get the "picture".

Below is an example of the previous main point, which utilizes both a simile and a metaphor. Can you pick them out?

> *Many of the problems with baseball today can be directly attributed to the fact that salaries are too high. In 1994 the average salary of a baseball player went through the roof. These high salaries have created a baseball player today who is more like a corporate CEO than an athlete.*

- **Analogies** - An analogy, while not considered evidence, is still a powerful persuader. Like the example, an analogy helps to clarify and define a main point or idea by reinforcing it's meaning. The difference is that, while an example refers specifically to the main point, an analogy does not. In analogies, an attempt is made to clarify a main point by referring to a similar situation that may be more relevant to the audience. America's entry into World War I, for example, could be explained by use of a "schoolyard" analogy which would start something like this, *"If you were on a schoolyard and saw several of your best friends getting beat up by the school bully. . ."*. Here is our same example using an analogy:

> **Many of the problems with baseball today can be directly attributed to the fact that salaries are too high. In fact, if we applied the same salary structure to UAW workers making automobiles in Detroit as we do to baseball players, then anyone with more than 5 years seniority would end up making more money that the president of General Motors.**

Transition Statements

So far we have developed the presentation's Body, and made it consist of three or more main points. Each main point is clearly defined and adequately supported. Now, the final touch is the addition of transition statements to provide a bridge between these main points. Transition statements are important to the audience's comprehension of our presentation.

As the speaker, we have the benefit of knowing what the entire presentation looks like in advance. We know for example, how many main points are going to be made, and when the presentation shifts from one main point to another. Although the Opening may give the audience some "clues" as to what lies ahead, the listeners are, for the most part, in the dark as to what directions the presentation will take. Transition statements signal that you've completed one main point and are moving on to another.

Besides leading the audience smoothly forward to the next main point, transition statements accomplish two other objectives. First they act as a "signpost" giving the audience a sense of where the speaker is in the presentation. Secondly, transition statements serve to bring the audience's attention back to the presentation. Many times, particularly when the listeners are already in agreement with your current point, their minds may tend to wander to other things. A strongly worded transition statement focuses their attention back on you, as they anticipate your next main point. Another technique that I find very useful to increase the impact of my transition statements is to generate body movement that coincides with the change in main points. While discussing one point I may stand in the middle of the room, as I begin to present my transition statement, I may move several steps to my left or right. The change in body position gives yet another clue to the audience that something has changed, and it has. We have moved on to a new main point.

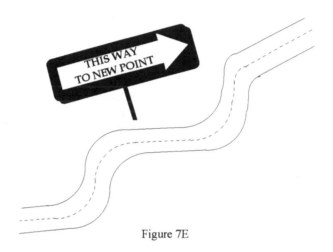

Figure 7E

The following are some examples of transition statements, notice how the "best" transitions recap the previous point while introducing the next point:

Good:

- *Let's begin by discussing our product's sales growth on the East Coast . . . .*
- *As we move to the Midwest, we find that this growth has. . . . .*
- *And finally, In the West we are not surprised to see that. . . . .*

Better:

- *One reason I believe in a strong defense is . . . .*

- *That's the first reason I believe in a strong defense, but there's another reason, and this is . . . .*

Best:

- *When it comes to Computer performance nobody is better than Unisys . . .*

- *. . . So when performance is an issue, you should think of Unisys, but you should also think of Unisys when price is a concern. Here's why. . . .*

PREPARING A PRESENTATION: A PRACTICAL EXAMPLE

On August 28, 1963, Dr. Martin Luther King gave what many people believe to be one of the greatest speeches of the twentieth century. In what has since been called his "I Have a Dream" speech, Dr. King was able to touch and inspire hundreds of thousands of people who had gathered in Washington D.C. for a peaceful civil rights march. The tremendous impact that this speech had is largely attributed to Dr. King's oratory style, which was impressive to say the least. What sometimes gets overlooked, however is that the speech, which lasted for less than 16 minutes, was almost perfect both in its organization and in it's simplicity.

It is fitting that a chapter on preparing a presentation should end with a quick look at some of the techniques Dr. King used in the organization of his most famous speech.

"I have a Dream" Speech

Topic:
Discuss the current state of Civil Rights in America

General Objective:
To inspire the audience to move ahead with a renewed enthusiasm regarding Civil Rights.

Specific Objective:
To discuss the past, present and future of the civil rights movement and motivate the listener to action

Main Points:

- Acknowledge America's historical "promise" of Equal Rights

- Current State of Civil Rights in America has fell short of that promise.

- Hope for the future and a call to action

Introduction

I am happy to join you today in what will go down in history as the greatest demonstration for freedom in the history of our nation.

Five score years ago, a great American, in whose symbolic shadow we stand today, signed the Emancipation Proclamation. This momentous decree came as a light of hope to millions of Negro slaves, who had been scared in the flames of withering injustice. It came as a joyous daybreak to end the long night of captivity.

But one hundred years later, the Negro still is not free, one hundred years later, the life of the Negro is still sadly crippled by the manacles of segregation and the chains of discrimination. One hundred years later, the Negro lives on a lonely island of poverty in the midst of a vast ocean of material prosperity. One hundred years later, the Negro is still languished in the corners of American society and finds himself an exile in his own land. And so we've come here today to dramatize a shameful condition.

Body

In a sense we've come to our nations Capitol to cash a check. When the architects of our republic wrote the magnificent words of the constitution and the Declaration of Independence, they were signing a promissory note to which every American was to fall heir. This note was a promise that all men-yes black men as well as white men-would be guaranteed the unalienable rights of life, liberty, and the pursuit of happiness.

It is obvious today that America has defaulted on this promissory note insofar as her citizens of color are concerned. Instead of honoring this sacred obligation. America has given the Negro people a bad check-a check which has come back marked "insufficient funds".

But we refuse to believe that the bank of justice is bankrupt. We refuse to believe that there are insufficient funds in the great vault of opportunity of this nation. And we've come to cash this check-a check that will give us upon demand the riches of freedom and the security of justice.

The first sentence acknowledges the importance of the event

Interest is created by addressing a common belief systems of the audience

The main points of the speech are then introduced in a King-like style

Notice the repetitive phrasing as each point is introduced.

A speech like this, that is designed to inspire, usually makes good use of metaphores

The "check" comparison is carried over several of the speech's main points

We have also come to this hallowed spot to remind America of the fierce urgency of now. This is no time to engage in the luxury of cooling off or to take the tranquillizing drug of gradualism. Now is the time to make real the promises of democracy. Now is the time to rise from the dark and desolate valley of segration to the sunlit path of racial justice. Now is the time to lift our nation from the quicksands of racial injustice to the solid rock of brotherhood. Now is the time to make justice a reality for all of God's children.

It would be fatal for the nation to overlook the urgency of the moment. This sweltering summer of the Negro's legitimate discontent will not pass until there is an invigorating autumn of freedom and equality. Nineteen Sixty-three is not an end, but a beginning. Those who hope that the Negro needed to blow off steam and will now be content will have a rude awakening if the nation returns to business as usual. There will be neither rest nor tranquillity in America until the Negro is granted his citizenship rights. The whirlwinds of revolt will continue to shake the foundations of our nation until the bright day of justice emerges.

But there is something that I must say to my people, who stand on the warm threshold which leads to the palace of justice. In the process of gaining our rightful place, we must not be guilty of wrongful deeds. Let us not seek to satisfy our thirst for freedom by drinking from the cup of bitterness and hatred.

We must forever conduct our struggle on the high plane of dignity and discipline. We must not allow our creative protest to degenerate into physical violence. Again and again we must rise to the majestic heights of meeting physical force with soul force.

The Marvelous new military which has engulfed the Negro community must not lead us to a distrust of all white people. For many of our white brothers, as evidenced by their presence here today, have come to realize that their destiny is tied up with our destiny. They have come to realize that their freedom is inextricably bound to our freedom. We cannot walk alone.

Body

The final main point is a call to action that takes on many different forms in the next six paragraphs.

Body

As we walk, we must make the pledge that we shall always march ahead. We cannot turn back. There are those who are asking the devotes of civil rights, "Wen will you be satisfied?" We can never be satisfied as long as the Negro is the victim of the unspeakable horrors of police brutality. We can never be satisfied as long as our bodies, heavy with the fatigue of travel, cannot gain lodging in the motels of the highways and the hotels of the cities. We cannot be satisfied as long as a Negro's basic mobility is from a smaller ghetto to a larger one. We can never be satisfied as long as a Negro in Mississippi cannot vote and a Negro in New York believes he has nothing for which to vote. No, no, we cannot be satisfied, and we will not be satisfied until justice rolls down like waters, and righteousness like a mighty stream.

I am not unmindful that some of you have come here out of great trials and tribulations. Some of you have come fresh from narrow jail cells. Some of you have come from areas where your quest for freedom left you battered by the storms of persecution and staggered by the winds of police brutality. You have been the veterans of creative suffering. Continue to work with the faith that unearned suffering is redemptive.

Close

Go back to Mississippi, go back to Alabama, go back to South Carolina, go back to Georgia, go back to Louisiana, go back to the slums and ghettos of our Northern cities. Knowing that somehow this situation can and will be changed. Let us not wallow in the valley of despair.

I say to you today, my friends, so even though we face the difficulties of today and tomorrow. I still have a dream. It is a dream deeply rooted in the American dream.

I have a dream that one day this nation will rise up and live out the true meaning of its creed, "We hold these truths to be self-evident, that all men are created equal."

I have a dream that one day on the read hills of Georgia the sons of former slaves and the sons of former slaveowners will be able to sit down together at the table of brotherhood.

The most important part of a speech whose purpose is to inspire, is the closing

In his closing, Dr. King begins by "Personalizing" his message to each listener.

The closing of a speech must be able to stand on it's own.

In this speech, the close stand on it's own so well that many people think that it was, itself, the entire speech.

Close

I have a dream that one day even the state of Mississippi, a state sweltering with the heat of injustice, sweltering with the heat of oppression, will be transformed into an oasis of freedom and justice.

I have a dream that my four little children will one day live in a nation where they will not be judged by the color of their skin but by the content of their character. I have a dream today.

I have a dream that one day down in Alabama, with its vicious racists, with its governor having his lips dripping with the words of interposition and nullification, one day right there in Alabama little black boys and black girls will be able to join hands with little white boys and white girls as sisters and brothers. I have a dream today.

I have a dream that one day every valley shall be exalted, every hill and mountain made low, the rough places will be made plane and the crooked places will be made straight, and the glory of the Lord shall be revealed, and all flesh shall see it together.

This is our hope. This is the faith that I go back to the South with. With this faith we will be able to transform the jangling discords of our nation into a beautiful symphony of brotherhood. With this faith we will be able to work together, to struggle together, to go to jail together, to stand up for freedom together, knowing that we will be free one day.

This will be the day - this will be the day when all God's children will be able to sing with new meaning. "My country 'tis of thee, sweet land of liberty, of thee I sing. Land where my fathers died, land where of the pilgrim's pride, from every mountainside, let freedom ring." And if America is to be a great nation, this must become true.

So let freedom ring from the prodigious hilltops of New Hampshire. Let freedom ring from the mighty mountains of New York. Let freedom ring from the heightening Alleghenies of Pennsylvania!

Let freedom ring from the snowcapped Rockies of Colorado! Let freedom ring from the curvaceous slopes of California!

The closing of a speech must also contain a memorable statement. . . .

. . . . Take your pick from the many memorable statements which are contained in the final paragraphs.

CHAPTER 8

PERSONALIZING THE PRESENTATION

By applying the principles outlined in Chapters 6 and 7 you have provided yourself with an excellent foundation for your presentation. You have selected a subject and done the required research. You have developed both an outstanding *Opening* and a dynamic *Close*. You have defined and expanded on the three to five key points that make up the presentation's *Body*, and you have organized these points in such a way as to maximize their effectiveness within the presentation. After all this, you may now ask yourself, "What's left? Is there anything more to creating an effective presentation?" The answer is *YES*, a lot more. You have the "words", but what the presentation lacks is a personality - *your personality*.

It is an unfortunate fact of life in the speaking profession that information alone cannot guarantee a presentation's effectiveness. No matter how effectively you've constructed the substance of the presentation it will be wasted if you fail to present it in an interesting manner. After all, what good is developing a presentation that has been designed to inform, persuade, inspire or entertain, if no one listens. Keeping the audience's interest is a necessity to making any presentation effective.

This chapter contains information that will help make the presentation you've developed more interesting and exciting. I refer to this process as personalizing the presentation. Personalizing the presentation requires you to add a little of yourself to the material. This may come in the form of humor, personal stories, and experiences. When you make a presentation your own, you make it more interesting and therefore more meaningful to both you and to your audience.

IMPORTANCE OF CREATING EXCITEMENT

Almost always the audience's attention and interest level are high as you begin your presentation. This is only natural, an audience is always willing to give a speaker the "benefit of the doubt" at the start of a presentation. In a very short time however, probably before you even finish your *Opening*, the attention of the audience can no longer be taken for granted. There is a natural tendency for the audience's attention to decline. This decline is due in part to the fact that while the human brain can comprehend the meaning of words at a rate of 450 - 600 words per minute, the average speaker only speaks between 120 - 150 words per minute. This leaves the listener's brain "idle" approximately 75% of the time. When the listener is interested in the presentation this "idle" time poses little problem and the brain waits patiently to process the next input. When the listener begins to lose interest, however, the brain may try to process other information during these "idle" states. Before long the brain is processing information which it feels is more worthwhile, such as what to have for supper that night, how late the dry cleaners is open, or maybe even planning when to take the car in for service. Let's face it, a presentation must compete for that 75% idle time within each individual listener. It is the presenter who can make the presentation interesting and exciting that has the best chance at keeping the listener's attention.

I have found several "sure-fire" ways to make a presentation more exciting, and they can all be grouped into the following five categories:

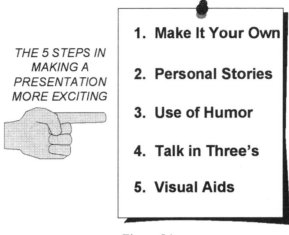

THE 5 STEPS IN MAKING A PRESENTATION MORE EXCITING

1. **Make It Your Own**

2. **Personal Stories**

3. **Use of Humor**

4. **Talk in Three's**

5. **Visual Aids**

Figure 8A

MAKE IT YOUR OWN

Although the term "exciting" is hard to define and may have different meanings to different people, there is one sure bet, it is extremely difficult to be exciting if you're just reading someone else's words. A presentation is not finished, and therefore should not be delivered until you *make it your own*. It was Ronald Reagan who summed it up best during a speech celebrating his 84th birthday in 1994 when he said:

> *"Speech delivery counts for little on the world stage unless you have convictions and, yes, the vision to see beyond the front row seats."*

What former President Reagan said is the essence of "*making it your own*". A presentation must be delivered with conviction and purpose to be truly interesting and energetic. Effective speakers understand that their role must be more than just that of the messenger, the message must be *theirs*. This also happens to be GOLDEN POINT #7.

Figure 8B

When you make a presentation "your own", you tend to present the information with more passion and conviction. This passion is first sensed, and soon shared, by the listener. Once the listener is caught up in *your* passion, then the excitement you wish to create is much more likely to be achieved. Recently, I attended a speech given by a former Dallas Cowboy wide receiver. The text of the speech was motivational in nature and talked about his rise to prominence as a local Dallas businessman. The former football player mostly read from a script and generated very little excitement with the audience. That is, until he stepped away from the podium, ignored his "prepared" remarks, and began telling stories from his football experiences. At that point he was a completely different speaker. His enthusiasm and excitement ignited the audience. He was telling *his* story, and each listener was drawn back into the presentation.

This is the very reason that some of today's most effective speakers come from the ministry, where for years they spoke about a topic that they had a passion about. Speakers like Jesse Jackson, Martin Luther King, and Billy Graham had little trouble translating that passion into politics or anything else they desired.

PERSONAL STORIES

If you're ever lucky enough to attend a motivational speech or sales seminar presented by Zig Ziglar, I can guarantee you that you will come away with all the motivation or salesmanship you can handle. I can also guarantee you that you will come away with a lot more than you expected. You will come away with images of what it's like to grow up in Yazoo City, Mississippi, what it's like to sell cookware door to door and what its like being married to that "redhead" of his for nearly fifty years. You will come away with stories about political figures and sports figures so vivid that you'll almost think they happened to you. Zig Ziglar is the master of personal stories.

Zig Ziglar knows what all good presenters know, that personal stories may be the single strongest tool in making presentations come alive for the audience. Relating stories or trivia to the audience that is of a personal nature allows the presenter to accomplish several objectives. Besides breathing life into the presentation it also sends a signal to the audience that you have an emotional stake in the material Knowing that you have experiences will tend to build both rapport and creditability with the listener, as well as keeping the interest level high.

Personal stories provide a good counterbalance within a presentation that is otherwise full of statistics or other highly technical material. A personal story may be a welcome break for the listener, particularly when the presenter has provided a significant amount of data for the audience to consume.

Finally, there is a hidden advantage to the use of personal stories. They require far less preparation than the rest of the presentation, and for the most part can be delivered in an impromptu manner (or at least look that way to the listener). During my years as a classroom instructor I kept detailed lesson plans of my lectures. When I reached that part of the lesson where I had intended to relate a personal story, the lesson plan may just read *"Tell story about first trip to IBM"*. With those seven words I could leave the podium and provide several minutes of "ad-lib" dialog. Dialog which came easy since it was of a personal nature.

A Personal story is intended to support a point within the body of the presentation. As with all other supporting material, it needs to be relevant, interesting and if possible, humorous. When personal stories are used correctly don't be surprised to find that they are remembered by the listener long after the points of the presentation are long forgotten.

USE OF HUMOR

Humor is a double-edged sword, which can be used to enliven a presentation or can instead be its downfall. When humor is used successfully it is by far the easiest method of establishing rapport with the listener. It can ease tension, enhance the speaker's image, and motivate the listener all at the same time. Humor makes the audience "feel good", and when the audience "feels good" they are more responsive to what you have to say. It is also widely accepted that when you mix the main points of the presentation with humor, they become easier to understand and more memorable.

When Humor is not used successfully however, it can have quite an opposite effect. Humor that goes awry can actually increase the speaker's tension and potentially damage any rapport that the speaker has already established with the listener. Because of this, humor should be used with considerable caution.

While there are no hard and fast rules relating to humor, it's affects can be maximized by adhering to the following guidelines:

- **Make it to the point** - Never forget that the primary job of the speaker is to convey a message. Humor can, and should be an effective part of that message. Resist telling that Joke you heard yesterday, just because it's funny. Instead, integrate humor into the subject of your presentation. Use it as a way of supporting your points. That way, if by chance the audience should fail to laugh, you're not left "holding the bag". You can instead make an easy transition back into your topic.

  Additionally, avoid setting up humor with such overused phrases as " *That reminds me of a story about . . .* ", or "*A funny thing happened . . .*". Humor is much more effective when it comes as a surprise to the audience.

- **Go for smiles not laughs** - In today's world of satellite communications, never has entertainment been so abundantly available to anyone who wants it. Cable TV and movies have exposed all of us to the best comedians and funniest moments of the past and present. Comedy is truly an art form and most speakers will have trouble competing on the same level as professionals. Unless the goal of the presentation is to entertain, it is probably better to leave the big laughs to the experts. Go for smiles and chuckles and your presentation will be better because of it.

- **Make it personal** - In developing presentations, we have talked about the need to make it your own. Never is this truer than with the use of humor. Humor works best when it is personal and natural. Endeavor to work from your own strengths. Shy away form jokes that require you to use dialects unless that is something that you are particularly adept at. Instead take humorous stories from either your own experiences, or situations that you have personally observed. This will allow *your* humor to be more natural.

- **Make it Brief** - There is nothing worse than an unfunny joke. Generally in humor, the longer the joke, the funnier it has to be. One-liners, humorous quotations, and witty remarks that are blended into the presentation can be just as effective as any long joke, but without the danger of disrupting the presentation if it should be met with silence.

SPEAK IN THREE's

When it comes to making a presentation that is both interesting and easily understood by the listener, there seems to be something irresistible about the number three. Studies have shown that, down through the ages, the most memorable parts of speeches tend to be grouped in three's. Take for example some of the following excerpts of which I am sure you are familiar:

> **Friends, Romans, countrymen lend me your ears . . . . .**
>
> **A government of the people, by the people, and for the people. . .**
>
> **I came, I saw, I conquered . . . .**
>
> **Free at last, free at last, thank God almighty I'm free at last . . . . .**

Pay particular attention to TV commercials that are designed by experts to appeal to the average listener. More often than not they will speak about the product in three's. A well known aspirin may be described as being *"safe, effective, and reliable. . ."* while a hair conditioner is said to *"fortify, nourish, and protect your hair"*.

Finally, pay special attention to a politician the next time that he is asked a "open ended" question such as "what are your qualifications for office?" More often than not he will only site three reasons in response to the question.

While I am sure that a grouping consisting of either two's or four's may be equally as appropriate in some situations, the important point to take from this is that any list should be limited to a small number. Nothing is more demanding on a listener than to try to both follow and remember a presentation which targets the *"14 ways to reduce your taxes"* or the *"11 traits of successful manager"*.

USE OF VISUAL AIDS

When it comes to supporting the points given in a presentation, nothing does it better than the use of visual aids. A picture may not *really* be worth a thousand words as the old Chinese proverb claims, but it's close. Use of visual aids can have a significant impact on the effectiveness of any presentation. As the picture below shows, of all the information we have acquired since birth, the vast majority of it has come to us visually. In fact, the sense of sight contributes over six times as much information as the sense of hearing.

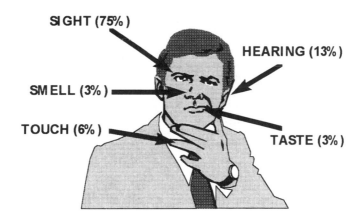

Figure 8C

Let's face it, we are "visual" by nature. Any presentation that combines a visual element along with a strong verbal message will be a better presentation. Visual aids enhance a presentation in two ways. First, by focusing the audience's attention and generating their interest. Secondly, by making the points in the presentation both easier to understand and remember. Let's take a closer look at these two benefits:

- **Focus Attention and Generate Interest** - A visual aid by its very nature commands the audience's attention. When a presenter uses visual aids within a presentation it has a tendency to focus the listener immediately on the point being supported. That point becomes more important to the listener simply because of the use of the visual aid.

  Ronald Reagan certainly used this technique in establishing his reputation as *"the great communicator"*. Even the Democrats were impressed by Reagan's first televised budget speech in which he used a handful of small change to illustrate the current value of a dollar. But that was small in comparison to his State-of-the-Union speech given in 1988. In that speech President Reagan admonished Congress on it's overly complex budget by temporarily stopping his speech and placing the budget resolutions on the table in front of him. When he finished, the pile stood over three feet tall and weighed over 43 pounds. Afterward, when President Reagan said, *"Congress shouldn't send another one of these. No -- and if you do, I will not sign it."* You can be sure he had everyone's attention.

- **Improve comprehension and retention** - Visual aids also help the audience understand and remember the ideas that are being presented, especially if those ideas tend to be highly abstract in nature. Consider some of the better programs being offered today to enhance a person's memory retention. These programs mostly utilize "visualization" techniques as a method to remember names, dates and places.

The people who develop these courses know better than anyone, the results of the study shown below in figure 8D:

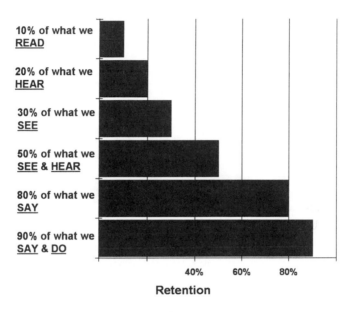

Figure 8D

This study shows a significant increase in retention to a listener who both sees and hears a point.

- **Enhance the delivery** - You may be asking, "What does visual aids have to do with enhancing my delivery?". The answer is simple - *NOTES!* Besides offering those benefits to the audience discussed above, visual aids provide an outline that you can speak from. In many of the "sales" presentations I have given, the visual aids (in the form of slides or overheads) may be the *only* notes I work from. If the visual aids are constructed correctly, and delivered effectively, they can constitute a complete presentation on their own. One warning however. Using visual aids to guide you through a presentation does not reduce the amount of preparation and rehearsal time that is required. In far too many presentations I have seen a speaker put up a slide, speak from it, and then bring up the next slide as if he were seeing it for the first time. Know the order of the visual aids and practice them in order. Keep in mind that using visual aids to deliver the main points of a presentation require the same use of "transition statements" that was discussed in chapter 7.

CHAPTER 9

PRACTICING THE PRESENTATION

This should be the shortest chapter in the book since the one thing that you can do that will influence a presentation's effectiveness the most, can be summed up in just three words: *Practice . . . . Practice . . . Practice.*

When Peggy Fleming took to the ice in the 1968 Winter Olympics, she had a tremendous amount of confidence, and it showed. Peggy Fleming's confidence did not come because she felt she had superior ice skating talents (although she probably did). Her confidence did not come from the fact that she was the reigning World Champion (although in fact she was). Peggy Fleming's confidence came from knowing that she had developed an outstanding routine, and also knowing that she could perform that routine flawlessly. Peggy Fleming indeed had the confidence that can only come through practice.

Although figure skating and giving a presentation are about as far apart as you can get, they are still similar in many ways. Giving a presentation, like performing an ice skating routine is only as good as the practice that went into it.

PRACTICE TECHNIQUE

The popular phase promises that "practice makes perfect". This is only partially true. What the phrase should really say is "*proper* practice makes perfect". There is a right-way and wrong-way to practice. Clearly, Peggy Fleming would not have been as prepared as she was, if she had just practiced her "jumps" but not her "spins". What if she had practiced both, but failed to do it to the music that she had decided to use? Would it be an effective practice? Of course not! You get the maximum effect from practice when you do the right things, the right way, and in the right order. When it comes to public speaking, I find that the following six steps provide the proper basis for practicing a presentation:

THE 6 STEPS TO EFFECTIVELY PRACTICE A PRESENTATION

1. **Read the Presentation Aloud**

2. **Study the Presentation**

3. **Prepare a Speaking Outline**

4. **Practice Your Speaking Outline**

5. **Practice Your Delivery**

6. **Dress Rehearsal**

Figure 9A

STEP 1:
READ YOUR PRESENTATION ALOUD

It is assumed that during the preparation process, you developed some sort of written document representing the presentation. This document may range anywhere from a list of notes and key phrases, all the way to a complete manuscript. Regardless of its form, the document should contain at the very least an *Opening*, a *Closing*, and a *Body* consisting of the key points of the presentation along with their appropriate supporting materials. The first step in practicing your presentation is to read this document aloud, as if you were giving the presentation itself. Don't worry if the presentation seems a little unpolished, you will take care of that latter. The purpose of reading the words aloud is to get a sense of the flow and rhythm of the presentation. Does the presentation sound like you expect it to? Do the ideas contained in the presentation sound clear and well organized? Are the words that you use easy to pronounced and easy to understand? Do the Opening and Closing accomplish their purpose? It's a fact that there is a significant difference between the way a presentation *"reads"* and the way it *"sounds"*. Use this first step to critically listen to what you have written and revise the presentation if necessary so that it *"sounds"* as good as it *"reads"*. After these revisions take place you will be left with a final version of the presentation.

STEP 2:
STUDY THE PRESENTATION

You have spent considerable time designing your presentation, and writing what you want. But do you really know what you've written? There is no use trying to work on your delivery until you fully know what it is you plan to deliver. Much like preparing for a biology test back in high school you will have to sit and study. Make note cards if you need to and study them whenever possible. Study your presentation sitting at a desk, riding in a car, or just lying in bed before you go to sleep.

Here's what you need to achieve through study:

- **Memorize the *Opening* and *Closing*** - You should never go into a presentation "winging" the *Opening* or *Closing*.

- **Know the Main Points** - Nor should you attempt to practice the presentation until you know all the main points and the order in which they appear.

- **Know the Supporting Material** - Once you begin your presentation it is too late to fumble for the statistics, illustrations, or quotations that you researched, a little study before hand can save considerable embarrassment.

STEP 3:
PREPARE A SPEAKING OUTLINE

The number one fear in the minds of singers is that they will sing off-key. A Golfer may dread the possibility of missing a three foot putt. While bowlers worry that they might throw a gutter ball. With a speaker it's the fear *of "drawing a blank"* - standing in front of an audience and suddenly forgetting what to say next. The purpose of a speaking outline is to prevent this from happening.

Early in the preparation phase, you may have made a rough draft of the points you wish to include into the presentation, you may even have written them in outline form. This however is quite different from a speaking outline. A speaking outline, as its name implies, is a guide to help the speaker advance step-by-step through the presentation. It provides the speaker with various cues for recalling key elements and phrasing that is part of the prepared text.

Once you have settled on the final form of your presentation, and have studied it satisfactorily, it's time to begin to prepare the speaking outline. The rules for establishing this outline will vary, not only from speaker to speaker, but from presentation to presentation. The speaking outline should be written to provide key words and phrases necessary to trigger your memory. At a minimum It should contain a lead-in to both the

Opening and *Closing*; the or five key words for each of the main points of the presentation; an indication of when a visual aid is to be use; any statistics you might need, especially if its important that those statistics be totally accurate; and finally, anything else you feel is significant to the success of the presentation.

Make sure that the speaking outline is as easy to read as possible. Keep it brief, too many words may destroy the whole concept of the outline. You need to be able to get what you want from the outline with just a glance. It is ineffective if you have to "read" what's on it. Similarly, the larger the print the better you can pick up the information with just one glance.

If I were in a situation where I was presenting "Step 3: Prepare a Speaking Outline" to a group, and decided to create a speaking outline to help me with that presentation. It might look something like this:

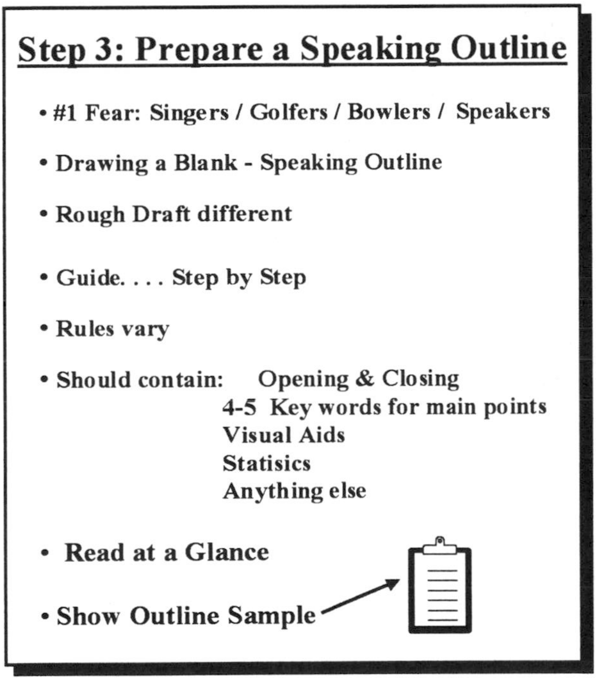

Step 3: Prepare a Speaking Outline

- #1 Fear: Singers / Golfers / Bowlers / Speakers

- Drawing a Blank - Speaking Outline

- Rough Draft different

- Guide. . . . Step by Step

- Rules vary

- Should contain: Opening & Closing
               4-5 Key words for main points
               Visual Aids
               Statisics
               Anything else

- Read at a Glance

- Show Outline Sample

Figure 9B

STEP 4:
PRACTICE YOUR OUTLINE ALOUD

How effective is your Speaking Outline? Does it provide the intended cues for you to follow? These questions are answered as you begin to practice with the outline. The more you practice with the speaking outline, the more familiar it will seem to you. By the time you are ready to deliver your presentation, one glance at the speaking outline should allow you to speak for several minutes without having to look down again.

It is important that, as you practice this speaking outline, you do it aloud. Remember, you are not just practicing the outline, *you are practicing the presentation*. Make sure your practice includes the entire presentation. This includes "talking through" all examples and adequately recounting all quotes and statistics. Pay particular attention to how the outline provides you with keys to your transition statements, since they were probably not a big part of your study so far. You will know when you have practiced the outline enough when you can go through the entire presentation without stumbling over any words or ideas.

STEP 5:
PRACTICE YOUR DELIVERY

Now you can begin to polish and refine your delivery. Practice your presentation as if you were giving it to an audience. Use your Speaking outline for support, but only as needed. Here you need to bring all phases of the presentation (the verbal, the vocal and the visual) together for the first time. You may elect to practice in front of a mirror to see how you are coming across to an audience. You may also want to tape record these practices to gauge your volume, rate, inflection and use of pauses. The best measure of your presentation however, comes from people. Whenever possible try to find an audience that can give you an instant appraisal. Keep in mind, your presentation was written for people not mirrors and tape recorders.

After practicing your delivery anywhere from three to six times you should feel considerable confidence, and ready to go. Before you do, however, that is one more final step to perform.

STEP 6:
DRESS REHEARSAL

The best way to do a dress rehearsal is to duplicate, as best you can, the conditions of your presentation. In fact, the dress rehearsal has such an impact on the outcome of the presentation, that it becomes our GOLDEN POINT #8

GOLDEN POINT #8:

WHENEVER POSSIBLE, PERFORM A COMPLETE DRESS REHEARSAL

Figure 9C

A dress rehearsal means using all your visual aids and, if possible rehearsing in the actual room that you will be speaking. I understand that sometimes it is not always possible be in the exact room. If you can't, then find one that closely resembles it. Be sure to understand the environment that you will be speaking in. Will there be a podium or lectern? What equipment will be provided for your visual aids (slide projector, overhead projector, flip chart, etc.)? Then do your dress rehearsal in this environment.

You shouldn't need more than one "run through" during the dress rehearsal. That is unless you run into problems that need to be ironed out. If you followed the previous five steps religiously, then this dress rehearsal should be a confidence builder. One more technique to reduce your tension and make you the best speaker you can be.

SUMMARY

Practicing the presentation is not just for the novice, it's for everyone. In May of 1996, the then Senate majority leader Bob Dole made a speech in which he resigned from the Senate in order to run for the Presidency of the United States. Although the speech lasted less than 10 minutes, it was rumored that Senator Dole spent most of the day rewriting and practicing the speech, including at least three full dress rehearsals within the room where the speech was to take place. These rehearsals were viewed by some of his closest aids who provided feedback in the form of suggestions. If someone, who had spent so much of his life speaking in public, places so much importance on the power of practice, can the rest of us take it for granted?

APPENDIX A

GOLDEN POINT REVIEW

GOLDEN POINT #1

GOLDEN POINT #1:

AN EFFECTIVE PRESENTATION IS ONE IN WHICH THE LISTENER BOTH RECEIVES AND UNDERSTANDS THE SPEAKER'S MESSAGE

CHAPTER
#1

PAGE 7

GOLDEN POINT #2

CHAPTER #2

PAGE 17

GOLDEN POINT #3

CHAPTER #3

PAGE 31

GOLDEN POINT #4

CHAPTER #5

PAGE 57

GOLDEN POINT #5

CHAPTER #6

PAGE 74

GOLDEN POINT #6

CHAPTER #7

PAGE 92

GOLDEN POINT #7

CHAPTER 8

PAGE 116

GOLDEN POINT #8

CHAPTER #9

PAGE 131

APPENDIX B

REVIEW OF
CONTENT LISTS

LIST #1

*THE 6 STEPS IN
PLANNING A
PRESENTATION*

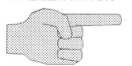

1. Determine The Topic

2. Decide What You Want
   To Achieve

3. Analyze The Audience
   And Setting

4. Research The Topic

5. Organize The Material

6. Focus The Topic

**CHAPTER
6**

PAGE 60

LIST #2

THE 4 STEPS IN PREPARING A PRESENTATION

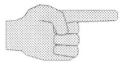

1. Organize The Body

2. Develop The Close

3. Develop The Opening

4. Develop The Body

CHAPTER #7

PAGE 74

LIST #3

THE 5 STEPS IN MAKING A PRESENTATION MORE EXCITING

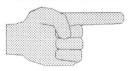

1. Make It Your Own

2. Personal Stories

3. Use of Humor

4. Talk in Three's

5. Visual Aids

CHAPTER #8

PAGE 99

LIST #4

THE 6 STEPS TO EFFECTIVELY PRACTICE A PRESENTATION

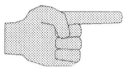

1. **Read the Presentation Aloud**
2. **Study the Presentation**
3. **Prepare a Speaking Outline**
4. **Practice Your Speaking Outline**
5. **Practice Your Delivery**
6. **Dress Rehearsal**

CHAPTER #9

PAGE 109

INDEX

NOTES

NOTES

NOTES

NOTES

NOTES